Planning to Teach Writing

Written by an experienced teacher and literacy consultant, *Planning to Teach Writing* offers an easy-to-use, tried-and-tested framework that will reduce teachers' planning time while raising standards in writing. Using the circles planning approach, it provides fresh inspiration for teachers who want to engage and enthuse their pupils, with exciting and varied hooks into writing, including picture books, short stories, novels and films.

Exploring effective assessment practice, each chapter puts the needs and interests of pupils at the forefront of planning, and models how to design units of work that will lead to high-quality writing outcomes in any primary school classroom.

The book uses a simple formula for success:

1 Find the gaps in learning for your students.
2 Choose a hook that you know will engage your students.
3 Select a unit plan that you know will support you to get the best writing out of your students.
4 Tailor it.
5 Teach it!

With a fantastic range of hooks to inspire teaching and learning, *Planning to Teach Writing* ensures successful planning that will maximise engagement, enjoyment and achievement. This book is an accessible and necessary resource for any teacher planning to teach writing in their classroom.

Emma Caulfield is an independent literacy consultant and teacher. She works in a variety of settings supporting schools to improve attainment and achievement in reading and writing; working alongside literacy leaders developing their strategic approaches, through to NQTs bedding in their practice and developing their subject knowledge.

Planning to Teach Writing

A practical guide for primary school teachers

Emma Caulfield

Routledge
Taylor & Francis Group

LONDON AND NEW YORK

First published 2016
by Routledge
2 Park Square, Milton Park, Abingdon, Oxon OX14 4RN

and by Routledge
711 Third Avenue, New York, NY 10017

Routledge is an imprint of the Taylor & Francis Group, an informa business

British Library Cataloguing in Publication Data
A catalogue record for this book is available from the British Library

Library of Congress Cataloging in Publication Data
Names: Caulfield, Emma, author.
   Title: Planning to teach writing: a practical guide for primary school teachers/Emma Caulfield.
   Description: Abingdon, Oxon; New York, NY Routledge, 2016.
   Identifiers: LCCN 2015034284| ISBN 9781138844407 (hardback) | ISBN 9781138844414 (paperback) | ISBN 9781315730394 (e-book)
   Subjects: LCSH: Composition (Language arts) – Study and teaching (Primary) | Creative writing (Primary education) | English language – Composition and Exercises – Study and teaching (Primary) | BISAC: EDUCATION/General.
   Classification: LCC LB1528. C38 2016 | DDC 372.62/3 – dc23
   LC record available at http://lccn.loc.gov/2015034284

ISBN: 978-1-138-84440-7 (hbk)
ISBN: 978-1-138-84441-4 (pbk)
ISBN: 978-1-315-73039-4 (ebk)

Typeset in Helvetica
by Florence Production Ltd, Stoodleigh, Devon, UK

This book is dedicated,
first, to my wonderful family for their
endless love and support.

I'd also like to mention my Reception
teacher, Diana Doudian, who inspired me
to be a teacher.

Finally, I'd like to thank Tony Martin
for teaching me a lot about great training and
engaging writers, and for encouraging me
to write this book.

Contents

CHAPTER 3
Using short films as hooks   **155**

Preface

This book will help teachers to produce effective unit plans for writing, and in doing so they will be able to concentrate on the core business of teaching units that help children to fulfil their potential as writers.

I have been in education since 1990 when I started my teaching degree at Liverpool Hope University (was LIHE). That year, an inspirational English tutor, Jean Clarkson, put us into pairs and asked us to read picture books to one another. That was it. My love affair with picture books began. Ever since that day, I have used books to inspire learners over and over again.

The visual image and how it can be used to inspire and engage children became the focus of my master's thesis (in 2005); this time, it was in the form of films and pictures. My research told me that using visual images to stimulate writing engaged almost all writers, and in particular lower-achieving writers.

By then, I was a literacy consultant working solely to support primary schools in their plight to improve achievement in reading and writing. I discovered that while many teachers knew what would engage learners, they did not know how to use the hooks within a broader teaching sequence.

In response to this, I developed tools and training packages to support teachers with planning sequences of work that led to rapid and sustained improvement in the writing achievement of pupils. However, in many cases, these sequences were not having the impact that they should, as teachers were not focused enough, in the initial planning stages, on what their pupils needed to improve on. It was clear that brilliant teaching was not leading to successful learning.

So, by bringing the elements of the well-known cycle of 'assess, plan, teach, assess' together, I found that writing achievement improved, rapidly. It was necessary to spend time supporting teachers with both assessment and planning; the more I did, the more I realised that it wasn't rocket science and *everyone* should know how to do this. Vitally, in addition to raising standards of achievement, this approach was cutting teachers' workload.

It is a fact that there is a direct correlation between standards of literacy and quality and longevity of adult life. The primary school teacher's role within this cannot and should not be underestimated; it is my hope that this book will help them to inspire and engage learners so that they can be the best writers possible.

Introduction

Effective composition involves articulating and communicating ideas, and then organising them coherently for a reader. This requires clarity, awareness of the audience, purpose and context and an increasingly wide knowledge of vocabulary and grammar. Writing also depends on fluent, legible and, eventually speedy handwriting.

(National Curriculum 2014)

The curriculum gives us a framework to follow – a guide to what we, as teachers in the classroom in England, are required to teach. Often, the curriculum is divided up, for example by year group, or by theme – composition, spelling, handwriting, etc., but teachers *have* to use their professional knowledge and skills to decide what, within the curriculum, their pupils can already do and what they already know, and what they still need to learn. Without this, the teacher will be covering the curriculum but not actually teaching it.

Figure 1 demonstrates how the curriculum and the teacher's knowledge of the pupils' learning come together, with knowledge of pedagogy, to create the optimum pedagogic approach. It is my belief that without 'knowledge of child', the teacher is likely to have little impact on learning. One area within this knowledge is where the child is up to in his or her learning.

Assessment is the key tool that teachers use to help them to decide where pupils are up to. The summative assessments ('assessment *of* learning') check how much and what learning has taken place after a period of teaching, whereas the formative assessments ('assessment *for* learning') provide an ongoing, often daily picture of where pupils' learning is up to. In 2002, the Assessment Reform Group said that 'Assessment for learning is fundamental to the development of independent learners . . . "the process of seeking and interpreting evidence for use by learners and their teachers to decide where the learners are in their learning, where they need to go and how best to get there"'.

I fundamentally and absolutely agree that assessment for learning is an essential part of a teacher's daily work. A teacher is always thinking 'has he or she understood that?' and 'where does he or she need to go next?' and 'do I need to go back over that again for pupil *x* or *y*?' However, when it comes to teaching writing, exclusively using Assessment for Learning to drive

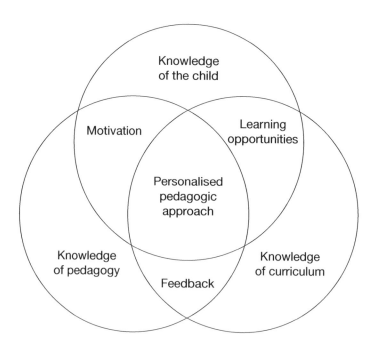

Figure 1 Combined knowledge needed to personalise learning in a classroom
Source: Dudley (2011: 208)

teaching can lead to teaching being reactive and fragmented. This means that planned units of work skim the surface of learning without embedding it; for example, they may teach children about the use of longer sentences for description without progressing them as writers by addressing a specific learning point, for individual pupils or groups of pupils, within 'long sentences'.

To take the example further: during teaching of a narrative unit, I may mark the children's drafts and find that many children are not using their punctuation accurately. I make a mental note to do some more teaching about punctuation within the next unit; or I may even put the teaching sequence for narrative writing on hold while I spend a couple of sessions on punctuation. Hence, as the teacher, I am reacting to issues as they emerge, and fragmenting the teaching of the narrative unit by dropping in 'other bits'.

The premise of this book is that a teacher's summative assessment of a pupil's writing is what should drive their planning. If, towards the end of each term, they analyse the range of writing that each child, or group of children writing at the same level as one another, then they can decide on the 'high tariff' areas that will need learning, developing or consolidating during the following term. In doing so, the teacher is strategically planning units of work, being proactive as opposed to reactive. Of course, once delivering those units, he or she will be using the information gathered on a daily basis to tweak teaching or address misconceptions; nevertheless, it is the summative assessment that drives the teaching.

Considering Figure 1 and 'knowledge of child', I have discussed the learning needs of pupils vis-à-vis writing, and will expand on this shortly; however, it is also important to remember that it is essential to tap into the interests of pupils in order to truly engage them in writing: 'We write best about what we know and what matters' (Corbett 2012). In order to find out what children know about and what matters to them, we need to get to know more about our pupils than simply how they perform in tasks. Additionally, once we know what interests them, it is also important to set up genuinely meaningful writing opportunities:

Pupils' experience in English extended beyond the classroom. They did this first through the provision of rich extra-curricular experiences outside school . . . Classroom activities involved real tasks, purposes, audiences and issues related to the local or wider community. In this way, the curriculum matched pupils' needs and interests.

(Ofsted 2011)

Gathering assessment information: finding the gaps

As a starting point, you will need some robust assessments of your pupils as writers – regardless of what system you are using to record your assessments, the following process relies on the teacher having a clear record of what each pupil can do in writing, and therefore highlights what he or she needs to develop or learn next. Your assessment system will reflect the writing curriculum as you will be measuring achievement against curriculum expectations.

I have suggested that gaps in writing are identified in three discrete areas: (1) word structure and language; (2) text structure; and (3) sentence structure and punctuation. For later-stage emergent writers or children who are beginning to write sentences, it would be more appropriate to look for gaps in spelling and handwriting than in text structure; therefore, the grid should, of course, be adapted to reflect the needs of the writers.

As many schools today, in England, have their own, individual assessment systems it is impossible to provide a catch-all pro forma for teachers to use. I have provided a model that can be adapted. Additionally, in order to save time, I suggest that assessment information that is later going to be harnessed and used to drive teaching is taken from a 'best-fit' child from each attainment group. This is based on the knowledge that, broadly, a pupil working at, for example, expected attainment for the end of Key Stage 1 will have similar strengths as another pupil working at the same level.

The process of gathering assessment information each term in order to identify gaps in learning is as follows:

1   Identify the pupil who best represents the attainment group's strengths and weaknesses in writing.
2   Collect his or her assessment information (e.g. from performance descriptors, or school's own attainment measures, or criterion scale) and approximately five pieces of recent, independent writing (i.e. completed by the child without adult intervention) from a range of different text types.
3   Using your assessment information, identify the broad areas of concern.
4   For each concern, look over the writing samples to identify the key issue.
5   Once you have recorded five or six key issues, decide on what you are going to teach to help to develop these areas of learning (teaching objectives).
6   For each issue, decide on a child-friendly target (learning outcomes).

NB: This process refers to children grouped according to the same writing attainment; it can, of course, be done with individual pupils too.

A quick guide to completing gaps sheets, a gaps sheet template and examples of completed gaps sheets can be found in the appendix.

Plugging the gaps

Once you know what you need to teach, you are one-third of the way there! Planning a teaching sequence that leads to improvement in writing (both plugging of gaps and consolidation of skills) is the next step, and of course teaching is the final stage.

Finally

Through using exciting and varied hooks into writing, this book provides inspiration for teachers who want to engage and enthuse their pupils. For each hook, there are suggestions of at least four different text types – these are in the form of mind maps – and three worked unit plans.

To get the best out of this book, follow these simple steps:

1 Find the gaps in learning for your students (as set out above).
2 Choose a hook (picture book, film/still, short story or novel) that you know will engage your students.
3 Select a unit plan that you know will support you to get the best writing out of your students.
4 Tailor it (add direct teaching elements that are needed).
5 Teach!

When you have used a few of these mind maps and plans, you can begin to create your own using the templates provided.

The circles
planning approach

The approach to medium-term planning used in this book is centred on a model provided by the Primary National Strategies (PNS). This model was taken from Eve Bearne's excellently researched structure for planning as set out in the joint UKLA/PNS publication *Raising Boys' Achievements in Writing* (2004). Longer, extended units of work are planned following a sequence of first reading, then planning, and finally writing:

> Based on the work of Bearne (2002), the research recommended a structured sequence to planning where the children and teachers began by familiarising themselves with a text type, capturing ideas for their own writing followed by scaffolded writing experiences, resulting in independent written outcomes.
>
> (Corbett 2008)

Not only does this approach allow teachers to see the big picture of a unit before they start teaching; it also enables them to plan a rich and impactful learning journey. Additionally, as the broad view of teaching is clear in the teacher's head, he or she is better equipped to allow the unit to twist and turn according to the needs and interests of learners. The research findings in 2004 were:

> . . . a three-week block was a new way of working, which was challenging but was seen to reap considerable benefit. For example:
> . . . the slow build up to the writing objective really helped my young writers, particularly the boys who enjoyed the variety across time around one text.
> . . . identifying specific long term intentions for each unit . . . enabled them to work more flexibly and creatively as they travelled towards these intentions and prompted them to listen to the children more acutely in the process. In focusing on the writing end product, they explicitly 'built in more time to develop thinking and imagination' and 'planned for more time for the children to enact and perform'.

. . . a general sense of satisfaction in being able to cover short-term objectives within a longer time frame. Some felt that in the past, in trying to cover a range of short-term objectives, their work had been fragmented; they enjoyed what they perceived as increased flexibility to respond to the needs and interests of the children, whilst still being guided by the overall intention of the unit.

(UKLA/PNS 2004)

The strongest and most structured parts of my recommended model are the first two phases: the teaching and learning that builds up to the children drafting and shaping their writing. Once these parts are taught, the teacher will have a greater sense of how long he or she needs to give to the guided and supported part of 'the final write'. If the groundwork has been laid, then the children will have firm foundations upon which to build – they will find the writing easier and more successful. The UKLA/PNS (2004) study called this 'providing time to journey'; it found that:

A core issue emerged of a focus on less literal time allocated to writing, but more generative thinking time in the form of an extended enquiry through drama and visual approaches. This time was energetically spent in imaginative and engaging explorations of texts. Such time was significant as it allowed the teachers/practitioners to feel less hurried and to listen and learn more about individuals. It also meant that when the children did undertake writing they were unusually focused and sustained their commitment, persisting and completing their work.

The third phase of teaching and learning should also be mapped out so that the teacher has a sense of how the writing will progress over time. Two considerations may be whether they will ask the children to write in chunks, using teacher modelling to support as and when needed, or whether they will be drafting in one sitting and following it up with some redrafting over time. What we know is that providing space and time for children to develop a piece of writing leads to better quality writing:

Allowing time for the writing to develop and giving the learners space in which to develop their ideas and move slowly and gradually towards a final piece of writing . . . clearly influenced the quality of the final pieces and partly accounted for the raised standards in writing.

(UKLA/PNS 2004)

In most primary schools, there are long-term plans for literacy that record the coverage and content for each term of the year; there are medium-term plans that indicate the coverage and content for each block of work, or 'unit'; and there are daily plans.

Each circles plan covers what has come to be known as a 'unit' of work. The timescale for coverage of the unit will depend on the amount of teaching and learning that needs to be done and on the pace at which pupils learn. For example, a poetry unit on creating shape poems may span five lessons, or a narrative unit on creating a spooky story may span 15 lessons. Broadly, before the unit starts, the teacher will have a sense of how many lessons it will take for the children to complete the journey through the phases of learning; however, there must be flexibility so that parts of the journey are repeated or skipped, in response to pupil need.

The circles plan is made up of three phases. Each phase plays an equal and vital part in building up to a final written outcome. Progression through the phases should feel like a journey

TEACHING SEQUENCE FOR WRITING

PHASE 1

- Immersion in text
- Shared reading
- Enjoy, explore and respond to text
- Develop comprehension skills
- Identify language/genre features
- Collect writer's hints and vocabulary

PHASE 2

- Gather ideas
- Oral rehearsal
- Plan

PHASE 3

- Shared writing
- Teacher modelling
- Teacher scribing
- Supported composition
- Guided writing
- Independent writing
- Draft, revise, edit

Teaching Sequence for Writing

PHASE 1

Immersion in text

Shared reading

Enjoy, explore and respond to text

Develop comprehension skills

Identify language/genre features

Collect writer's   hints and vocabulary

Short Writing

Sentence Level Work

PHASE 2

Gather ideas

Oral rehearsal

Plan

Guided Groups

PHASE 3

Shared writing

Teacher modelling

Teacher scribing

Supported composition

Guided writing

Independent writing

Draft, revise, edit

Spelling and Vocabulary Work

for both pupils and teachers – a teaching journey for teachers and a learning journey for pupils. The journey should have twists and turns, there may even be diversions and delays, but the process itself should be enriching and engaging, and the final outcome, the destination, truly fulfilling.

The purpose of phase 1 is for the pupils to be immersed in text – the text type that they will eventually be authors of. The final outcome of phase 1 should always be that pupils know 'what a good one looks like' (WAGOLL) and, in many cases, 'sounds like' too. Phase 2 is the time for pupils to think about, plan, orally rehearse and play with their ideas for writing. And phase 3 is the writing phase. The journey begins at reading and ends with writing. This process is also known as (and rooted in) the 'teaching sequence for writing'.

We have already established that the teaching sequence for writing has three phases that are discrete yet linked, which is why it is presented as a Venn diagram (see page xiv). We also know that the sequence is a map that guides teaching through a journey, of which the final destination is a piece of writing. The sequence is just that – a guide – it is the big picture of a unit of work; it should not be followed to the letter (the detail of teaching will be in the daily planning), but flex in response to pupils' learning. Equally, there are no timescales attached to the sequence. Some units may take a week of lessons to deliver; others may take three weeks.

Phase 1: immersion in text type

AIM OF PHASE 1: TO KNOW WHAT A GOOD ONE LOOKS AND SOUNDS LIKE

A simple fact that cannot be argued with is that it is very difficult to write a particular text type if you are not familiar with it. Familiarisation with the text type is the first step, by the end of phase 1 children should be so immersed in it that they could write it if they had to. In *The Really Useful Literacy Book*, Martin *et al.* (2004: 39–41) say that:

> writers have to have read the text type they are trying to write or have it read to them . . . From the experience of being read to and then wide reading, the writer builds ideas of what a successful piece of writing looks and sounds like . . . Children need to read and read and read – in order to both absorb the structures, sentence constructions and vocabulary of written texts . . .

Immersion is done through shared reading, when the teacher acts as a model reader making overt what good readers do by, for example, paying attention to the punctuation, using expression and intonation to aid understanding and bring the text alive, and asking him or herself questions and predicting. Pupils should always be able to see and follow the text during shared reading.

Shared reading is an opportunity to examine the purpose and audience of text, as this will be very useful when pupils begin to write their own: 'if we add together purpose and audience (why am I writing and who will be reading it?) we find ourselves considering the best ways to construct the text we want to write' (Martin *et al.* 2004: 34).

In addition to, and during, shared reading, the text should be brought alive so that children engage with it, understand it and respond to it as readers. It is really important that children are given opportunities to explore their responses to text; as children engage in 'booktalk', an expression coined by Aidan Chambers in his *Tell Me* approach (1993), they are experiencing being the audience – understanding how it feels to make sense of, and respond emotionally to, what they are reading. The purpose of this, within the teaching sequence for writing, is to help writers to begin to consider what response they may want to elicit in the reader. You can't truly write for an audience unless you've walked in the footsteps of the audience.

As well as eliciting reader response, immersion in the text enables children to hear and collect vocabulary and language patterns, internalise plot structures and deepen their understanding. At this point in phase 1, the children should be supported to gather vocabulary that they like and think they will utilise in their writing.

Equally, rather than the teacher giving the children a list of elements that feature in a text type, they should be collecting them as they read and engage in the text type. During phase 1, children should be given opportunities to collect, in addition to vocabulary, ideas and authorial effects to be used, later, in their own compositions. These lists are sometimes referred to as 'success criteria' or similar; however, it is my belief that the more child-friendly, less threatening, labels such as 'writer's hints' make more sense to children, and therefore are more likely to be used when they write. These lists can be used as checklists during or after writing, but they should always be displayed, perhaps on a 'working wall', during the unit.

Booktalk and close analysis of the text, this time focusing on *how* the writer has achieved effects on the reader, and being supported to understand what the writer has done to elicit this response and have that effect, are also key parts of phase 1 of the teaching sequence. These ideas should be added to the 'writer's hints' list mentioned above.

Phase 2: gathering ideas and shaping them into a plan

AIM OF PHASE 2: TO HAVE PLANNED MY WRITING

In order to be ready to compose a text, we need to have collected ideas, played with them, decided on the best ones and then shaped them into some form of a plan. This is what phase 2 is for.

Initially, experimentation is the key – children should be freed up so that the ideas flow. They should be encouraged to share ideas, identify what might work, play with vocabulary and language so that they can find the best way to express themselves, and orally rehearse. All of these methods involve talk. Ros Fisher *et al.* (2010: 39) state that 'talk will help them think up and extend their ideas but also . . . help them to gain a better understanding of the writing task set by the teacher'. She explores using talk to generate ideas through role-play, drawing on experience, using pictures and artefacts, and telling others.

In his *Talk for Writing* approach, Pie Corbett (2008: 6–7) suggests the use of:

- Writer-talk games . . . to develop and focus aspects of ideas and language for writing
- Word and language games to stimulate the imagination and develop vocabulary and the use of language
- Role play and drama to explore ideas, themes and aspects of the developing writing

Once children have had opportunities to talk through their ideas, they should then be shaped into a plan. This may be a story map, mountain or a storyboard, a series of boxes or a skeleton. It is my opinion that schools should have set planning pro forma so that pupils become familiar with the format; I also believe that planning formats should be the same for all text types.

Phase 3: extended write/completion of whole text

AIM OF PHASE 3: TO HAVE DRAFTED AND REFINED A PIECE OF WRITING

Once children 'know' the text type (from phase 1) and have planned their own (in phase 2), they should be ready to write. The first step of phase 3 is to support the children to get started on their writing through shared writing. Shared and guided writing are the only opportunities a teacher has to truly teach writing. Shared writing has three elements: teacher modelling, teacher scribing and supported composition.

When a teacher models writing, he or she is demonstrating, and making explicit, what a writer does when he or she composes. Narrating as he or she goes, the teacher shows the pupils how to write; how to use the plan and writer's hints to support with structuring the writing and ideas; and how to orally rehearse sentences, reread and edit 'on the run'. Acting as a scribe in 'teacher scribing', the teacher takes ideas from the children and shapes them into a piece of writing. He or she does this by focusing pupils on the texts they have been immersed in, the writer's hints and the plan; helping them to generate ideas and selecting the most appropriate or powerful; and balancing his or her 'expert' skills with the pupils' developing knowledge to produce a good-quality written piece.

'Supported composition' can act as the bridge between modelled writing and independent writing. It provides the pupils with an opportunity to 'have a go' on mini-whiteboards (or similar) while in a supportive environment. During supported composition, the teacher supports writers by providing the stimulus and challenge, and picking up on misconceptions, while the pupils write. Often, the pupils will only be writing a small amount – perhaps a sentence or two; they will then share and refine their writing and take it away with them as a starting point for independent work.

Shared writing is usually carried out as a whole-class activity. Small group work or 'guided writing' is another feature of phase 3 (although guided work should also be woven through phases 1 and 2). This is the time for a teacher to work with a small group on a specific aspect of their writing; it may be around sentence or paragraph development, or language use, or it may have a broader focus such as text structure or editing. The importance of taking the time to work with small groups cannot be overemphasised. For many busy primary practitioners, this really is the *only* time that pupils are taught specific writing skills in a targeted way – done well, it has the most impact on the quality of children's writing.

Independent writing can and should only be expected from pupils once they have been equipped with the skills and knowledge needed to do so successfully. Many teachers wonder and debate with colleagues how independent a final piece is if the pupils have been given support in writing it. To me, this is simply 'teaching'! If I give a child the knowledge, skills and confidence to write independently, and he or she goes off and writes independently (using some of the ideas and strategies as support), then he or she is indeed an 'independent' writer.

The final part of any 'good' writing is checking and editing. The English National Curriculum (2014) states that it is an end of KS2 requirement for children to be able to:

Evaluate and edit by:
- assessing the effectiveness of their own and others' writing and suggesting improvements
- proposing changes to grammar and vocabulary to improve consistency, including the accurate use of pronouns in sentences
- proof-read for spelling and punctuation errors

Polishing writing to ensure that it communicates exactly what and how the writer intended is a vital skill for children to be taught, regardless of these statutory elements; therefore, it should always be included in phase 3.

Other elements that are woven through the phases

In addition to, and integral to, the teaching content of the three phases, there are short writes, guided group work and word/sentence teaching. All of these are a fundamental part of the teaching sequence; without them, the quality of the final written outcomes and subsequent attempts at the same text type may be disappointing as learning will not be deep enough.

Throughout phases 1 and 2, short writing opportunities should be planned. These may vary in length, from writing up new vocabulary into journals through to paragraphs of information or narrative. Short writes keep children writing! They allow children to practise what they have been taught, record ideas and exercise their writing muscles.

The benefits of guided writing have already been mentioned. Once the activities for the phases are planned, the teacher should identify a group to work with during each activity. The focus of the session will depend on the children in the group and what they need; for example, during phase 1, a group may need support with using effective vocabulary (that they have collected) or with a specific sentence level issue, and during phase 2, they may need support with creating a plan or preparing questions for hot-seating.

Finally, word/sentence teaching needs to be identified during the phases and planned for; this gives the teacher an opportunity to contextualise word/sentence learning for children. Usually, the sentence level focus will be dictated by the needs of the children; direct teaching may be done in discrete slots followed by opportunities to practise new skills and knowledge during the unit of work. For example, if children need to be able to use commas to mark clauses, during phase 1 they might be identifying commas and discussing the 'job' that they do in sentences. Then the teacher may do a direct teach about commas to mark clauses. This would be followed by some sentence games to practise the new knowledge.

In phase 2, the teacher may plan some more practice activities so that children can 'play' with commas to mark clauses, and then in phase 3 he or she can ensure that the use of commas to mark clauses is demonstrated during shared writing.

Similarly, spelling and vocabulary learning should be referred to and practised during the unit, wherever possible.

The hook

The best tool that a teacher has in his or her toolkit is the one that hooks the children into writing. Once engaged, children will want to write and will write well. In her blog about the use of video, drama and real-life experience as hooks into writing, Parietti (2013) said: '. . . using these [ideas and approaches] as hooks and new ways to stimulate the children, gets them excited in a lesson and it's this excitement and engagement that means they'll achieve the most'.

Powerful texts (novels, short stories, poems, comic strips and picture books) can all provide superb hooks into writing: 'If . . . we use powerful texts as the basis of our literacy teaching, we stand the best chance of motivating children to undertake the work' (Martin et al. 2004: 12). They go on to say that 'In their research in London with Year 5 children published as 'The Reader in the Writer' (2001), Myra Barrs and Valerie Cork . . . suggest that the reading of powerful texts was one of the key factors responsible for children producing high quality writing' (Martin *et al.* 2004: 12).

A hook can be used right at the start of a unit, or it may be better to put it in at the end of phase 1 – once the pupils have been immersed in the text type – so as to stimulate ideas in phase 2. For example, if children are going to be writing their own versions of the David Wiesner story *Tuesday* (which is about frogs flying!), the hook could go in at the start: a trail of lily pads could be dotted about the classroom. If they are going to write newspaper articles about flying frogs, then the hook could go in after phase 1 (when they are familiar with the newspaper article text type) in the form of the book being shared.

Hooks can be huge and exciting or small and enticing. It is up to the teacher to plan the right hook for the children and indeed the text type.

How to complete a circles plan

You will naturally have two starting points to a unit plan. One is to know what text type you are going to teach and the other is to know what knowledge and skills you are teaching in order to improve the children's writing. Be careful; if the text-type you have chosen does not help you to teach the parts that will improve your pupils' writing, change the text type!

1   Start by planning the final outcome (what you want the children to have produced at the end of the unit). What will it be? Be specific; for example, 'an information page for a class book' is better than 'an information text'. Now add onto it what knowledge/skills you are looking to develop through the text type, for example well-structured paragraphs or effective use of inverted commas for dialogue or use of commas to mark clauses. If you do this, your final outcome should always be:

   ● **To write a** [specific text type goes here] **with** [two specific writing knowledge/skills to be improved go here].

   For example, **write an information leaflet with a clear structure and technical vocabulary**. The areas to develop are generic for the class; later, when you come to complete your daily plans, you will need to consider how these will be differentiated. Put simply, an example of differentiation for 'clear structure' is:

	Below-average writer	Average writer	Above-average writer
To use a clear structure in an information leaflet	To be able to group ideas into sections	To be able to use paragraphs to organise ideas in the leaflet	To use well-structured paragraphs to organise ideas in the leaflet

2   Complete the 'key focus' boxes for each phase. This remains the same for all three phases – it is the key areas that you are focusing on throughout the unit. The example here is 'clear structure and technical vocabulary'.

3   Plan the outcome for the end of phase 1. As the purpose of phase 1 is to immerse the pupils in the text type so that they know what a good one looks and sounds like, the outcome will be:

● **To know what a good** [specific text type goes here] **looks and sounds like.**

4   Plan the outcome for end of phase 2. As the purpose of phase 2 is to prepare the children for writing their own composition, the outcome will be:

● **I have planned my** [specific text type goes here].

5   List the activities that you would like to use to teach the aspects needed in phases 1, 2 and 3. Be as specific as you can; for example, 'shared read three information leaflets on . . .' or name the text and page numbers that you will share. In phase 2, 'hot-seat the zoo keeper to find out . . .'. For phase 3, you will need to map out how you think that the build-up to the independent write will go (this may change as you teach it, to flex with the children as their written outcomes evolve).

6   Go through your activities and check that you have put 'key focus' teaching and practice activities into each phase – remember that it is this teaching that will truly move your pupils' writing forward.

7   Go through the phase 1 and 2 activities and check that you have included 'short writes'.

8   Consider audience and purpose for the writing, and where it will be published – it's up to you whether you write this onto the plan.

9   Finally, plan your hook. How will you hook the children into the writing? When will you put in the hook?

See Appendix F for a blank circles plan and circles planning quick guide.

Skeleton circles plan

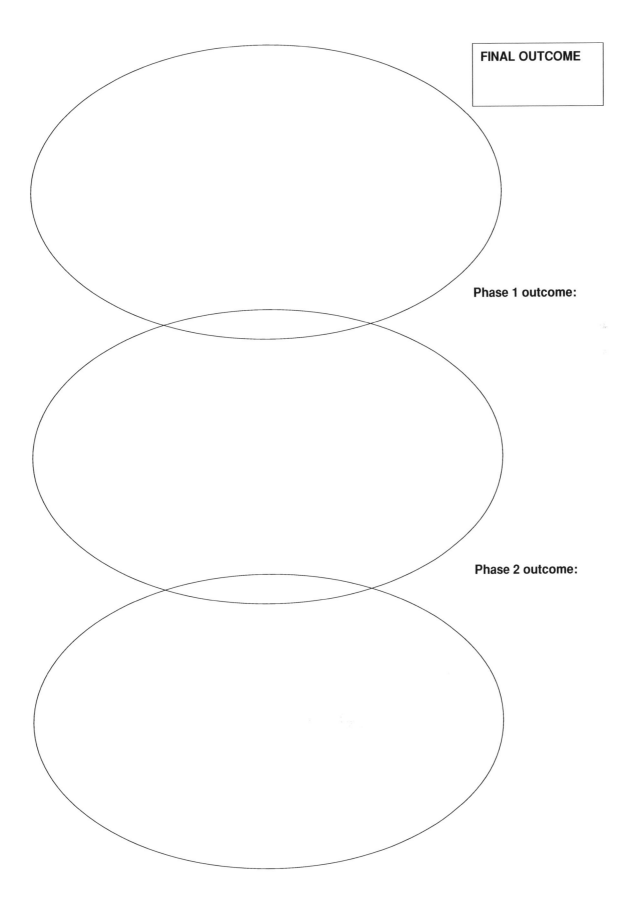

FINAL OUTCOME

Phase 1 outcome:

Phase 2 outcome:

Unit plans

Introduction

This chapter is divided into three subsections. Each is based on a different hook (see Chapter 1 about 'hooks') into writing: picture books, short stories and novels, and short films.

Within each subsection, divided into Key Stage 1 and Key Stage 2, there are:

(a) mind maps showing the different text types that could be stimulated by each hook; and
(b) circles plans that demonstrate how to reach the written outcomes and also that demonstrate that the 'hooks' can be used at different points during the teaching sequence.

The mind maps are to give you an idea of the breadth and scope of writing that can be stimulated by each 'hook'. Each map has suggestions for three or more of the following text types: narrative; description; instruction; recount; explanation; information; persuasion; discussion; poetry. Sometimes the suggested writing topic for non-fiction text types will cross over into fiction, for example a set of instructions for how to swim in a washing machine.

Each circles plan has a suggested year group or Key Stage; please note that these are only suggestions based on the age appropriateness of the hook, teachers may, of course, adapt and amend them to tailor them to their pupils.

Please find below explanations for some terms that are used in the circles plans:

Reader response – likes, dislikes, puzzles, patterns (usually phase 1)
Articulating responses to text helps children to decide what makes it effective. This is an activity that asks the children what they liked and disliked, any questions about it, and any patterns that they can see within the text or across other, similar texts.

Compare and contrast (phase 1)
This is where the teacher guides the pupils through a comparison of texts to identify similarities and differences, and, more importantly, which is more effective and why.

Mapping/story map/storyboard (phases 1 and 2)

A visual representation of text – usually small pictures – that are in chronological order.

Story mountain (phases 1 and 2)

A visual representation of the parts of a story that build up to the 'problem' from the opening, and then back down to the ending.

Writer's hints (phase 1)

Writer's hints (sometimes known as success criteria or checklists) are the identified aspects of text that the pupils may want to use when they write their own – the elements that they have agreed are effective. They are usually collected during phase 1 and should be displayed on a working wall. There should only be three or four hints for younger children and five or six for older.

Chunk the text or chunks (phases 1 and 2)

Separating the text into story or text parts – so that the children can see the underlying plot or text structure. The parts of a story are usually: opening; build-up; problem; resolution; ending. Non-fiction text parts vary. Planning for each chunk of text is suggested at phase 2.

Talk/word/language games (phases 1 and 2)

These provide an opportunity to 'talk the text' before writing. They usually occur when the children are gaining an understanding of the language used in certain text types, and are suggested as a fun way to keep the children tuned in to the appropriate words or language.

Orally rehearse (phase 2)

This is practising the sentences (or more) orally in order to say and hear them, and refine them if necessary, before writing.

Short stories and novels section

For each novel, it is assumed that the complete novel has been read to the class *before* the unit of work is begun, unless otherwise stated. For the novels and short stories, there are occasionally suggestions in the circles plans of places to stop reading in order to allow the children to predict what will come next – please do read the circles plans thoroughly before sharing the novel or short story with your class.

Short films section

At the time of writing, each film can be found on the Internet. There is a brief synopsis of each film in Appendix 9, and the URL for each is in the respective mind map.

CHAPTER 1

Using picture books as hooks

Mind maps
and unit plans

Captions/labels
Freeze-frame moments and put in thought bubbles; label spooky elements in illustrations; label the rooms in the castle and the items in each room

Instructions
How to get to the castle safely; warning notices/signs; route map/instructions; how to find the box

A Dark, Dark Tale
by
Ruth Brown

Narrative
Write your own dark, dark tale; write a bright, bright tale; describe the woods, moor, castle; predict and describe what's in the box

Poetry
Learn by heart, compose sound effects and perform; spooky poems; poems that have a contrasting theme (to darkness); cats; castles

Information
Tourist guides: castles, haunted houses, woods, moors; fact files: cats, toys, ghosts, woods, dark/light

UNIT PLAN

Theme: *A Dark, Dark Tale* – Instructions

Key Stage 1

PHASE 1

- Hook – read *A Dark, Dark Tale*
- Explain task – to write a set of instructions for how to get to the castle safely
- Shared read various sets of instructions
- Explore and respond – compare and contrast
- Identify the features and typical language of instructions (e.g. introduction, what you need, what you do, bossy verbs, ordered steps, concluding statement)
- Build list of writer's hints for instructions
- Play language games to develop understanding of bossy verb meanings (e.g. mime the action)
- Chunk text into sections and discuss layout (purpose)

FINAL OUTCOME
To write a set of instructions

Phase 1 outcome

To know what a good set of instructions looks and sounds like

PHASE 2

- Play games that involve the children giving instructions to each other
- Draw out the language and continue to build banks and understanding
- Reread *A Dark, Dark Tale* and use drama/role play to explore the instructions you might give for getting to the castle safely
- Use chunked set of instructions as basis for plan of new set
- Practise use of bossy verbs appropriate to this set of instructions
- Talk activities to support with ideas for what you might put into an introduction, and the 'what you need' section
- Talk activities to support with ideas for adding detail into each step (e.g. make sure that you stick to the path)
- Support with ideas for a concluding statement
- Complete plan

Phase 2 outcome

To have planned my instructions

PHASE 3

- Shared write introduction
- Children write introduction and 'what you need' independently
- Shared write initial steps
- Children write steps independently
- Shared write concluding statement
- Children complete independently
- Mark, feed back and edit
- Publish and share

UNIT PLAN

Theme: *A Dark, Dark Tale* – **Narrative**   Key Stage 1

FINAL OUTCOME
To write *A Bright, Bright Tale*

PHASE 1

- Read *A Dark, Dark Tale* and respond (likes, dislikes, puzzles, patterns)
- Map *A Dark, Dark Tale* onto a story mountain or map so that children can see the pattern and plot
- Collect effective language and vocabulary – check understanding of effect
- Build list of writer's hints

Phase 1 outcome
To know *A Dark, Dark Tale* and what makes it a good story

PHASE 2

- Discuss what *A Bright, Bright Tale* might be about
- Use picture stimulus to support ideas
- Use drama/role play to explore events or setting of *A Bright, Bright Tale*
- Collect vocabulary along the way
- Use story map or mountain to support with planning new tale
- Use word/language games to change vocabulary and language collected from *A Dark, Dark Tale* to *A Bright, Bright Tale*
- Explore new vocabulary
- Orally rehearse new ideas
- Finalise plan

Phase 2 outcome
To have planned my story

PHASE 3

- Show children mock-up of final book
- Model write opening – using story map or plan
- Children write opening independently
- Model write main events – using story map or plan
- Children write main events independently
- Model write ending – using story map or plan
- Children write ending independently
- Mark, feed back and edit
- Publish and share

UNIT PLAN

Theme: *A Dark, Dark Tale* – Poetry   Key Stage 1

FINAL OUTCOME

To write, publish and perform spooky spine poems

PHASE 1

- Read a range of spooky poems
- Explore and respond – which do you prefer and why?
- Learn a spine poem by heart
- Begin to collect writer's hints for what makes a good spooky spine poem
- Identify features
- Expand vocabulary by generating synonyms for dark and scary
- Introduce 'simile' and collect examples from poems read so far; add to writer's hints list
- Continually read similar poems to develop 'ear' for them

Phase 1 outcome

To know what good spooky poems are and to be able to retell/perform one

PHASE 2

- Choose a picture from *A Dark, Dark Tale*
- Collect key vocabulary
- Play word and language games to develop ideas, especially relevant similes
- Make sure that elements of writer's hints are explored in the context of ideas generated by *A Dark, Dark Tale*
- Plan spine poem
- Orally rehearse ideas
- Refine and/or develop them

Phase 2 outcome

To have planned my own spooky spine poem

PHASE 3

- Model how to use plan to write beginning of poem
- Recap expectations around adventurous vocabulary and use of similes
- Independent write of poems
- Publish poems
- Practise performing poems
- Share and perform poems
- Evaluate them

Recount
Postcards: from Beegu to her parents; to the 'small ones' on her return. Letters: to Beegu now that she is home; persuading parents/head teacher to keep Beegu

Description
Settings: Beegu's home/planet; the school, dogs home; characters: Beegu, her parents, other characters featured

Beegu

by Alexis Deacon

Instructions
For Beegu to follow: recipes, simple games, how to get home

Narrative
The story from Beegu's point of view; another Beegu adventure; write the ending (reunion with parents); Dialogue: thought/speech bubbles or play scripts from extracts of the story; translate Beegu

UNIT PLAN

Theme: *Beegu* – Instructions

Key Stage 1

FINAL OUTCOME

To write a set of instructions

PHASE 1

- Hook – read *Beegu*
- Explain task – to write a set of instructions for how to get home
- Shared read various sets of instructions
- Explore and respond – compare and contrast
- Identify the features and typical language of instructions (e.g. introduction, what you need, what you do, bossy verbs, ordered steps, concluding statement)
- Build list of writer's hints for instructions
- Play language games to develop understanding of bossy verb meanings (e.g. mime the action)
- Chunk text into sections and discuss layout (purpose)

Phase 1 outcome

To know what a good set of instructions looks and sounds like

PHASE 2

- Play games that involve the children giving instructions to each other
- Draw out the language and continue to build banks and understanding
- Reread *Beegu* and use drama/role play to explore the instructions you might give for her to get home
- Use chunked set of instructions as basis for plan of new set
- Practise use of bossy verbs appropriate to this set of instructions
- Talk activities to support with ideas for what you might put into an introduction, and the 'what you need' section
- Talk activities to support with ideas for adding detail into each step (e.g. make sure that you are properly strapped into your seat)
- Support with ideas for a concluding statement
- Complete plan

Phase 2 outcome

To have planned my instructions

PHASE 3

- Shared write introduction
- Children write introduction and 'what you need' independently
- Shared write initial steps
- Children write steps independently
- Shared write concluding statement
- Children complete independently
- Mark, feed back and edit
- Publish and share

UNIT PLAN

Theme: *Beegu* – Narrative   Key Stage 1

PHASE 1

- Hook – alien sighting on playground
- Front cover discussion
- Brainstorm Beegu character
- Read *Beegu* and respond (likes/dislikes/puzzles/patterns)
- Focus on the ending and analyse effects created by author; collect writer's hints
- Map out the ending using thought bubbles
- Read familiar stories; discuss alternative endings
- Map using thought bubbles then compare/contrast to *Beegu*

Phase 1 outcome

To know what makes a good ending and be familiar with the *Beegu* ending

PHASE 2

- Collect ideas for alternative endings (decide on audience)
- Map out
- Rehearse effective sentences that have an impact on reader
- Add thought bubbles to map – use drama to establish feelings/thoughts
- Collect and orally rehearse sentences and vocabulary
- Create storyboard plan

Phase 2 outcome

To have planned my alternative ending to *Beegu*

PHASE 3

- Shared write first paragraph of ending
- Independently write first paragraph
- Shared write final section
- Independently write final section
- Model how to review and improve writing
- Read to partner, review and improve writing
- Read whole story to chosen audience

UNIT PLAN

Theme: *Beegu* – Postcards

Key Stage 1

FINAL OUTCOME
To write postcards to and from Beegu

PHASE 1

- Hook – 'lost' poster from Beegu's parents
- Discussion about how the class could respond
- Shared read selection of postcards so that children immersed in language and structure
- Discuss various purposes/audiences
- Build list of writer's hints
- Use engaging stimuli to practise writing short, concise messages (bear purpose and audience in mind)
- Teach and practise grammar and punctuation elements needed for writing short, concise messages

Phase 1 outcome
To know what postcards are and how they are used to send short messages

PHASE 2

- Use drama/role play to explore what Beegu might want to say to her parents if she was to send them a postcard
- Orally rehearse
- Use drama/role play to explore what her parents might say in their reply to her postcard
- Orally rehearse

Phase 2 outcome
To have planned my postcards to and from Beegu

PHASE 3

- Shared write postcards to and from Beegu
- Independently write postcards to and from Beegu
- Revise and edit the postcards
- Introduce new hook (e.g. postcard from a child to Beegu)
- Practise independently writing postcards to new audience
- Edit and publish

Captions/labels
Draw one of the settings, label it; freeze-frame moments and put in captions; label items to pack in the suitcase; luggage labels

Lists
Things he should pack in his suitcase; things that might be in the lost and found office

Lost and Found by Oliver Jeffers

Narrative
The story from penguin's point of view; another adventure for the boy – perhaps he finds a giraffe at his door; write a sequel

Poetry
South Pole-inspired (e.g. snow, cold); penguins; friendship; journeys; our homes

Information
Penguin fact files; South Pole fact files or brochures; journeys; homes; caring for pets; looking after people

UNIT PLAN

Theme: *Lost and Found* – Penguin fact file

Key Stage 1

FINAL OUTCOME
To write a penguin fact file

PHASE 1

- Shared read a range of information texts/fact files
- Explore and respond – which do you prefer and why?
- Immerse the children in a range of fact files
- Build up a list of writer's hints
- Identify fact file features
- Collect technical vocabulary; add 'penguin'-related vocabulary
- Short write a fact file on whales/seals/similar animal (assess skills/knowledge)
- Address misconceptions

Phase 1 outcome

To know what a good fact file looks and sounds like

PHASE 2

- Provide stimulus for penguin fact file (hook)
- Explore key vocabulary
- Play word and language games to develop ideas
- Plan penguin fact file (including 'design' decisions)
- Orally rehearse ideas
- Refine and/or develop them

Phase 2 outcome

To have planned my own penguin fact file

PHASE 3

- Model how to use plan to write fact file introduction, and shared write
- Independent write of introductions
- Model how to use plan to write next part of fact file, and shared write
- Independent write of next parts
- Redraft elements that need polishing
- Publish

UNIT PLAN

Theme: *Lost and Found* – Narrative   Key Stage 1

FINAL OUTCOME

To write a sequel to *Lost and Found*

PHASE 1

- Read *Lost and Found* and respond (likes, dislikes, puzzles, patterns)
- Shared read stories with similar plot patterns
- Explore and respond – likes, dislikes, puzzles, patterns
- Collect writer's hints for these stories
- Use story map or mountain to chart the key events of *Lost and Found*
- Use drama/role play to understand key parts of the plot

Phase 1 outcome

To know the plot and narrative language in *Lost and Found*

PHASE 2

- Use picture or artefact stimulus to discuss other adventures that could be had – who might come to his door?
- Use drama/role play to explore new adventures – where would it lead? What would happen?
- Collect vocabulary along the way
- Replace main events on story map or mountain with new ideas
- Children create a new story map or plan
- Use word/language games to explore new vocabulary
- Orally rehearse new ideas
- Finalise plan

Phase 2 outcome

To have planned my sequel to *Lost and Found*

PHASE 3

- Show children mock-up of final book
- Model write opening – using story map/plan
- Children write opening independently
- Model write main events – using story map/plan
- Children write main events independently
- Model write ending – using story map/plan
- Children write ending independently
- Mark, feed back and edit
- Publish and share

UNIT PLAN

Theme: *Lost and Found* – Snow poems   Key Stage 1

FINAL OUTCOME
To write, publish and perform 'snow' poems

PHASE 1

- Read a range of winter/cold themed poems
- Explore and respond – which do you prefer and why?
- Learn a poem (similar to the final outcome) by heart
- Begin to collect writer's hints for what makes a good poem
- Identify features
- Expand vocabulary by generating synonyms for colours and size (e.g. 'emerald' instead of 'green'; 'tiny' instead of 'small')
- Introduce 'simile' and collect examples from poems read so far; add to list of hints
- Continually read similar poems to develop 'ear' for them

Phase 1 outcome
To know what good themed poems are and to be able to retell/perform one

PHASE 2

- Provide stimulus for snow poetry
- Explore key vocabulary
- Play word and language games to develop ideas, especially relevant similes
- Make sure that elements of the writer's hints are explored in the context of snow poetry
- Plan poem
- Orally rehearse ideas
- Refine and/or develop them

Phase 2 outcome
To have planned my own snow poem

PHASE 3

- Model how to use plan to write beginning of poem
- Recap expectations around adventurous vocabulary and use of similes
- Independent write of poems
- Publish poems
- Practise performing poems
- Share and perform poems
- Evaluate them

Persuasion
Letters asking Sunny to come home; adverts for the best place to live; safety posters (example in book); travel brochure page; invitations

Narrative
Tell the story; write one of the visits as a story; invent a new adventure for another meerkat; describe characters/settings

Meerkat Mail by Emily Gravett

Information
Fact files: meerkats, other animals; fact files or tourist guides: the Kalahari Desert, other places; travel guide/lists: what Sunny needs for travelling

Recount
Postcards; letters; diary entries; news reports (examples in book); holiday or journey scrapbook (journal) with captions

UNIT PLAN

Theme: *Meerkat Mail* – Narrative

Key Stage 1

FINAL OUTCOME

To write a story with repeated patterns based on *Meerkat Mail*

PHASE 1

- Read *Meerkat Mail* and respond (likes, dislikes, puzzles, patterns)
- Shared read stories with repeated patterns
- Explore and respond – likes, dislikes, puzzles, patterns
- Collect list of writer's hints for these stories
- Use a story map or mountain to chart key events of the story
- Use drama/role play to understand the key events

Phase 1 outcome

To know what a good story with repeated patterns sounds and looks like

PHASE 2

- Use picture or artefact stimulus to discuss other adventures that a meerkat could have – who might they visit and why might it not be suitable?
- Use drama/role play to explore new adventures
- Collect vocabulary along the way
- Replace main events on story map or mountain with new ideas
- Children create a new story map or plan
- Use word/language games to explore new vocabulary
- Orally rehearse new ideas
- Finalise plan

Phase 2 outcome

To have planned my story

PHASE 3

- Show children mock-up of final book
- Model write opening – using story map/plan
- Children write opening independently
- Model write main events – using story map/plan
- Children write main events independently
- Model write ending – using story map/plan
- Children write ending independently
- Mark, feed back and edit
- Publish and share

UNIT PLAN

Theme: *Meerkat Mail* – Postcards   Key Stage 1

FINAL OUTCOME
To write postcards to Sunny

PHASE 1

- Hook – *Meerkat Mail* postcards from Sunny
- Discussion about how the class could respond
- Read selection of postcards
- Discuss various purposes/audiences
- Build list of writer's hints
- Use engaging stimuli to practise writing short, concise messages (bear purpose and audience in mind)
- Teach and practise grammar and punctuation elements needed for writing short, concise messages

Phase 1 outcome
To know what postcards are and how they are used to send short messages

PHASE 2

- Use drama/role play to explore what Sunny's family might want to say if they were to send him a postcard
- Orally rehearse
- Practise using grammar and punctuation elements to make responses concise and clear

Phase 2 outcome
To have planned my postcards to Sunny

PHASE 3

- Shared write postcards to Sunny
- Independently write postcards to Sunny
- Revise and edit the postcards
- Publish

This process can be done for several postcards to Sunny. Children could also write Sunny's responses.

UNIT PLAN

Theme: *Meerkat Mail* – Persuasion (travel brochure)   Key Stage 1

FINAL OUTCOME
Travel brochure (persuasive information)

PHASE 1

- Read travel brochure extracts
- Help children to understand purpose and audience of each
- Immerse children in travel brochure
- Identify persuasive language used and collect
- Identify descriptive language used and collect
- Use model texts to look at structure of typical brochure extract (e.g. food, sights, where to stay)
- Build list of writer's hints
- Hook – another meerkat wants to visit one of the places – as a class, you have to write a brochure showing him the best place to go

Phase 1 outcome
To know what good travel brochure descriptions sound like

PHASE 2

- Agree purpose of class brochure (audience is a new meerkat)
- Use talk activities to explore content
- Plan three sections – food, sights, places to stay (for each section, support children with ideas)
- Practise use of descriptive vocabulary
- Plan other elements that may appear on the page (e.g. photos, maps, diagrams)

Phase 2 outcome
To have planned my travel brochure page

PHASE 3

- Shared write opening section
- Children write opening independently
- Shared write second section
- Children write section 2 independently
- Shared write third section
- Children write section 3 independently
- Edit
- Share with pupils from other class and evaluate

Recount
Write the 'story' of the book as a recount; letters to/from each boy (or other characters) telling them about their day; a day in the life of me; diary entries; 'my journey' recount

Narrative
Tell and write the *Mirror* stories; invent magic carpet stories; research and write a new *Mirror* story

Mirror
by Jeannie Baker

Information
Morocco/Australia fact files; a contrasting country to my own fact file; about Arabic; carpet making; fair trade

Description
Describe any of the characters; the landscape or cityscape; the contrasting homes; artefacts

UNIT PLAN

Theme: *Mirror* – Fact file

Key Stage 1

FINAL OUTCOME
To write a fact file about a country based on *Mirror*

PHASE 1

- Read a range of information texts/fact files
- Explore and respond – which do you prefer and why?
- Immerse children in 'countries' (e.g. Morocco or Australia) fact files
- Collect list of writer's hints
- Identify fact file features
- Collect technical vocabulary
- Short write a fact file on a country (or city) you know to assess skills/knowledge
- Address misconceptions

Phase 1 outcome
To know what a good fact file looks and sounds like

PHASE 2

- Provide stimulus for the chosen country fact file (hook)
- Present children with key facts and fascinating facts
- Explore key vocabulary
- Play word and language games to develop ideas
- Plan fact file (including 'design' decisions)
- Orally rehearse ideas
- Refine and/or develop them

Phase 2 outcome
To have planned my own fact file

PHASE 3

- Model how to use plan to write fact file introduction, and shared write
- Independent write of introductions
- Model how to use plan to write next part of fact file, and shared write
- Independent write of next parts
- Redraft elements that need polishing
- Publish

UNIT PLAN

Theme: *Mirror* – **Narrative**   Key Stage 1

PHASE 1

- Shared read 'journey' and fantasy stories
- Explore and respond – likes, dislikes, puzzles, patterns
- Collect writer's hints for these stories
- Collect effective language and vocabulary
- Use a story map or mountain to chart the events of a simple magic carpet story
- Use drama/role play to understand key parts of the plot
- Add to vocabulary bank and writer's hints list

Phase 1 outcome
To know the plot of a good 'journey' story

PHASE 2

- Use *Mirror* to stimulate a discussion about a magic carpet
- Use drama/role play to explore new adventures – where would it lead and what would happen?
- Collect vocabulary along the way
- Replace main events on story map with new ideas, or demonstrate how to start planning
- Children create a new story map/plan
- Use word/language games to explore new vocabulary
- Orally rehearse new ideas
- Finalise plan

Phase 2 outcome
To have planned my magic carpet story

PHASE 3

- Show children mock-up of final book
- Model write opening – using story map/plan
- Children write opening independently
- Model write main events – using story map/plan
- Children write main events independently
- Model write ending – using story map/boxed up plan
- Children write ending independently
- Mark, feed back and edit
- Publish and share

UNIT PLAN

Theme: *Mirror* – Recount

Key Stage 1

FINAL OUTCOME
To write my own
Mirror recount

PHASE 1

- Hook – read and respond to *Mirror* (likes, dislikes, puzzles, patterns)
- Write a model recount to accompany one of the stories – either the Moroccan or the Australian family's story
- Play with the sentence structures and vocabulary in the model so that children are clear about this text type
- Chunk the model into key events – build a bank of vocabulary for each, and develop children's understanding of this vocabulary
- Use the model to support knowledge of structure and explore the use of time connectives
- Collect writer's hints for a recount

Phase 1 outcome
To know what a good
recount looks and
sounds like

PHASE 2

- Use the story chunks from phase 1 to support children to role-play a typical day for them
- Ask them to bring in photographs (before/after school events) and use a collection of photos to stimulate vocabulary
- Sequence the pictures and orally rehearse the use of time connectives
- Build a new plan of their own *Mirror* recount

Phase 2 outcome
To have planned my
Mirror recount

PHASE 3

- Show mock-up of own *Mirror* book and agree audience/purpose
- Shared write opening
- Children write opening independently
- Shared write middle sections
- Children write middle sections independently
- Edit and redraft as necessary
- Shared write endings
- Children write endings independently
- Mark, feed back and polish drafts
- Publish, share and evaluate

Information
Fact files/leaflets/Wikipedia
pages: nocturnal animals; barn owls;
other owls; dark/light; stars/
space/telescopes

Poetry
Themed by: owls; animals;
nocturnal animals; dark; fear;
fireworks; space; stars;
moon

The Owl Who Was Afraid of the Dark
by Jill Tomlinson

Narrative
Write your own
'afraid of the . . .' story; write
another adventure for Plop; add new
events to the story; write a story
about the dark; add thought
bubbles to key moments

Description
Write a description of Plop;
other owls; the firework display;
woods settings; trees; owl
nests; starry skies

UNIT PLAN

Theme: *The Owl Who Was Afraid of the Dark* – Setting descriptions   Key Stage 1

FINAL OUTCOME
To write two setting descriptions

PHASE 1

- Shared read known stories and use them to discuss what 'settings' are
- Shared read and immerse children in a variety of good-quality setting descriptions
- Collect list of writer's hints for setting descriptions
- Play word/language games to develop the language of description
- Chunk a setting description into parts so that children understand structure
- Hook – read *The Owl Who Was Afraid of the Dark* and respond (likes/dislikes/puzzles/patterns)
- Focus on the settings (forest, owl's nest, firework skies/forest) and collect vocabulary from the book

Phase 1 outcome
To know what a good setting description sounds like

PHASE 2

- Begin with the forest – use pictures from the book and other pictures/artefacts to build a picture of the setting
- Label with vocabulary; build a bank
- Support the children to create a plan for the setting description
- Pair work – children 'talk' their descriptions (use collected vocabulary effectively)
- Play word/language games to continue to develop and rehearse the language of description
- Carry out the same process as above but for the forest and sky during the fireworks

Phase 2 outcome
To have planned my two setting descriptions

PHASE 3

- For the forest: model write first couple of lines (including modelling how to work from a plan)
- Children independently write their descriptions
- Share and refine
- Children independently write their descriptions of the setting during the fireworks (putting into practice what they have learned from the forest descriptions)
- Edit, refine and publish

UNIT PLAN

Theme: *The Owl Who Was Afraid of the Dark* – Information page   Key Stage 1

FINAL OUTCOME
To write a page for a class information book

PHASE 1

- Read a range of information texts
- Explore and respond – which do you prefer and why? Purpose and audience of each?
- Immerse children in animal information texts
- Identify information page features (including visual elements such as pictures/diagrams)
- Collect technical vocabulary
- Collect list of writer's hints

Phase 1 outcome
To know what a good information page looks and sounds like

PHASE 2

- Provide stimulus for new animal information page (hook)
- Explore key vocabulary
- Play word and language games to develop ideas
- Plan information page (including 'design' decisions)
- Orally rehearse ideas
- Refine and/or develop them
- Check plan is complete

Phase 2 outcome
To have planned my information page

PHASE 3

- Model how to use plan to write introduction, and shared write
- Independent write of introductions
- Model how to use plan to write next part of information page, and shared write
- Independent write of next parts
- Redraft elements that need polishing
- Add visuals (e.g. photographs)
- Publish, share and evaluate

UNIT PLAN

Theme: *The Owl Who Was Afraid of the Dark* – Narrative

Key Stage 1

FINAL OUTCOME

To write *The . . . Who Was Afraid of the Dark* story

PHASE 1

- Read *The Owl Who Was Afraid of the Dark* and respond (likes, dislikes, puzzles, patterns)
- Chunk it into sections so that children can see the pattern and plot
- Reread *The Owl Who Was Afraid of the Dark* regularly until the children have internalised some of the language and sentence structures
- Collect effective vocabulary and language – check understanding of effect
- Build list of writer's hints

Phase 1 outcome

To know *The Owl Who Was Afraid of the Dark* story and what makes it a good story

PHASE 2

- Discuss another animal who it would be funny if they were afraid of the dark
- Use picture stimulus to support ideas
- Use drama/role play to explore new events
- Collect vocabulary along the way
- Map or plan new story
- Use word/language games to orally rehearse new vocabulary and language
- Orally rehearse new story
- Finalise plan

Phase 2 outcome

To have planned my story

PHASE 3

- Show children mock-up of final book
- Model write opening – using plan
- Children write opening independently
- Model write main events – using plan
- Children write main events independently
- Model write ending – using plan
- Children write ending independently
- Mark, feed back and edit
- Publish and share

Persuasion
Adverts for the zoo; leaflets about animals in captivity; letters against animals in captivity; code of conduct for visitors to the zoo

Narrative
Tell the story from the animals' point of view; innovate the story so that the family visits somewhere else; write part of the story as a play script; freeze-frame and add thought bubbles

Zoo
by Anthony Browne

Discussion
Are zoos good for animals?
Do humans need zoos?
Balanced news reports about zoos

Recount
The trip to the zoo; diary entry; a day in the life of an animal/zoo keeper at the zoo

UNIT PLAN

Theme: *Zoo* – Discussion

Key Stage 1

FINAL OUTCOME
To write a discussion about whether zoos are good for animals

PHASE 1

- Shared read a range of age-appropriate discussion texts
- Use talk activities to further explore the concept of 'discussion', including purpose and audience
- Immerse children in simple discussion texts so that they know some of the language by heart
- Check understanding of typical language/vocabulary
- Play language games to practise using simple discursive language and understand what makes it effective
- Collect list of writer's hints
- Chunk simple text into sections and discuss layout (purpose)
- Clarify structure of discussion texts (paragraphs: intro, points for, points against, conclusion) NB This is easier for children if the title is expressed as a question, e.g. 'Are zoos good for animals?'

Phase 1 outcome
To know what good discussion texts look and sound like

PHASE 2

- Reread *Zoo* – introduce hook into discussion title: 'Are zoos good for animals?' (e.g. local zoo closing)
- Use chunked text from phase 1 to start to plan new discussion
- Use discussion-based role-play and drama games to explore ideas for and against zoos being good for animals
- Use language games to further explore the effective use of discursive language
- Orally rehearse possible introductions/conclusions to this discussion
- Complete plan

Phase 2 outcome
To have planned my own discussion text

PHASE 3

- Shared write introduction and points for sections
- Children independently write introduction and points for sections
- Shared write points against and concluding sections
- Children independently write points against and concluding sections
- Support with editing and refining discussions
- Share and evaluate

UNIT PLAN

Theme: *Zoo* – Persuasion

Key Stage 1

FINAL OUTCOME
To write and perform a radio advert and write a persuasive leaflet

PHASE 1

- Shared read a range of age-appropriate leaflets advertising days out (e.g. safari parks, theme parks, farms, etc.)
- Use talk activities to further explore the concept of 'persuasion', including purpose and audience
- Immerse the children in persuasive leaflets so that they know some of the typical language structures by heart
- Collect writer's hints
- Play language games to practise using simple persuasive language
- Clarify structure of persuasive leaflets by chunking and discussing purpose

Phase 1 outcome
(1) To have performed a radio advert (2) To know what good persuasive leaflets look and sound like

PHASE 2

- Read *Zoo* – hook into task
- Use chunks from phase 1 to start to plan new persuasive leaflet about *Zoo* (or one that the children have visited)
- Use discussion-based role-play and drama games to explore ideas for elements that would persuade people to visit
- Use language games to further explore the effective use of persuasive language
- Complete plan
- Decide on visual and design elements to be included (e.g. special offer banner, photographs)

Phase 2 outcome
To have planned my own persuasive leaflet

PHASE 3

- Shared write first section
- Children independently write first section
- Mark/feed back and children edit/polish
- Shared write next section
- Children independently write next section
- Support with editing and refining
- Add final design elements (e.g. photographs)
- Publish
- Share and evaluate

UNIT PLAN

Theme: *Zoo* – **Play script**

Key Stage 1

FINAL OUTCOME
To write a play script based on *Zoo*

PHASE 1

- Shared read short plays (start with known stories, e.g. *Traditional Tales*)
- Discuss and check understanding of what a play script is – purpose and audience
- Children act out short scenes – turn them into short-burst play scripts by shared writing
- Shared read play scripts and analyse for features
- Build writer's hints for play scripts and magpie key vocabulary

Phase 1 outcome
To know what a play script is and the features of a good one

PHASE 2

- Hook – read *Zoo* and respond: likes, dislikes, puzzles, patterns
- Check children's understanding of story and underlying issues
- Choose a key scene – use drama to act out
- Freeze-frame and discuss how to record as a play script
- Collect vocabulary for narrations/stage directions
- Orally rehearse using writer's hints
- Map/plan play script

Phase 2 outcome
To have planned my play script

PHASE 3

- Shared write play script
- Children independently write play script
- Support with editing and refining
- Perform, share and evaluate

Mind maps
and unit plans

Explanation
How the . . . dragon got its . . .;
how to look after a dragon; why dragons are
extinct; how to catch a dragon

Description
Develop descriptions of
dragons using book as a starting
point; describe new amazing
creature

Tell Me a Dragon

by Jackie Morris

Poetry
Our own *Tell Me a Dragon*
collection; 'My Dragon' poem;
'My . . . (type of creature)'
poem

Information
Magazine report about
dragons, or a particular dragon;
dragon fact file/information
leaflet

Recount
Newspaper/broadcast
reports on dragon sightings;
extracts from a dragon
keeper's diary

UNIT PLAN

Theme: *Tell Me a Dragon* – Explanation

Lower Key Stage 2

FINAL OUTCOME

Explanation text
*How to Look After
a Dragon*

PHASE 1

- Shared read explanation texts
- Explore and respond, begin to build writer's hints list
- Immerse children in explanation texts
- Unpick language features and add key ones to writer's hints
- Discuss purpose and audience
- Build word bank of technical vocabulary (short write glossary) and other 'explanation'-type words/phrases
- Direct teach around the structure of the explanation text – heading, introduction, paragraph content, conclusion, diagrams/pictures
- Chunk text (e.g. *How to Look After a Dinosaur*) into sections and discuss layout (purpose)
- Introduce explanation task – hook
- Finalise list of writer's hints

Phase 1 outcome

To know what a good explanation text looks and sounds like

PHASE 2

- Use hook and picture/video stimulus to discuss technical vocabulary needed for writing explanation task
- Begin to build list of technical vocabulary
- Play word and language games to practise using 'explanation'-type words/phrases in context
- Map out new text and use drama/role play to explore sections
- Create new plan, including technical vocabulary to be used
- Make decisions about layout: what goes where on the page and why?

Phase 2 outcome

To have planned my explanation text

PHASE 3

- Model write introduction (including focus on vocabulary)
- Children write own
- Shared write first paragraph (including focus on vocabulary)
- Children write own
- Support with decisions about next paragraph, including layout
- Children complete the rest of their explanations
- Mark, feed back and edit (focus on structure and effective vocabulary)
- Publish and share

UNIT PLAN

Theme: *Tell Me a Dragon* – **Newspaper reports**   Lower Key Stage 2

FINAL OUTCOME
Newspaper report
'Dragon found . . .'

PHASE 1

- Hook – watch *Guardian* newspaper advert (3 Little Pigs)
- General discussion re: news – what does it mean and why do we need it?
- Shared read age-appropriate newspaper reports and respond
- Immerse children in newspaper reports so that they internalise the language patterns
- Discuss how stories are handled/portrayed
- Check understanding of purpose and audience of newspaper reports
- Collect list of writer's hints, and appropriate vocabulary
- Chunk newspaper report into sections to check understanding of typical structure

Phase 1 outcome

To know what a good newspaper report looks and sounds like

PHASE 2

- Introduce stimulus for 'Dragon found . . .' newspaper reports
- Begin to plan using the chunked report sections
- Explore key events through drama/freeze-framing and hot-seating
- Explore headline to use
- Orally rehearse use of journalistic language; record key ideas

Phase 2 outcome

To have planned my newspaper report

PHASE 3

- Shared write opening, including headline and use of language
- Children independently write openings
- Shared write next parts picking up on issues as report progresses
- Children independently write next parts
- Peer evaluate success, then edit
- Publish

UNIT PLAN

Theme: *Tell Me a Dragon* – Poetry

Lower Key Stage 2

FINAL OUTCOME
To write, publish and perform 'My Dragon' poems

PHASE 1

- Read a range of 'creature'-themed poems
- Explore and respond – which do you prefer and why?
- Learn a poem by heart
- Begin to collect list of writer's hints
- Identify features
- Introduce *Tell Me a Dragon* hook
- Read *Tell Me a Dragon* – provide opportunities for children to explore and respond
- Explore similes used, direct teach and play to develop knowledge and understanding of similes

Phase 1 outcome

To know what good themed poems are and to be able to retell/perform one

PHASE 2

- Introduce model 'My Dragon' poem
- Play language development games using pictures from *Tell Me a Dragon* to stimulate ideas
- Chunk 'My Dragon' poem and use as a basis for planning
- Children choose a dragon as the theme of their poem; using drama and language games to support idea development, children plan their own 'My Dragon' poem
- Play with similes to ensure that they're used to enhance the poetry

Phase 2 outcome

To have planned my own 'My Dragon' poem

PHASE 3

- Model how to use plan to write beginning of poem
- Recap expectations around adventurous vocabulary and use of similes
- Independent write of poems
- Publish poems
- Practise performing poems
- Share and perform poems
- Evaluate them

Information
Our stories; about immigration;
imaginary creatures; historical
information about immigration;
refugees today

Description
Add 'colour' to the pictures and
describe settings and characters;
describe the machines and creatures;
describe characters' feelings
at key moments

The Arrival
by Shaun Tan

Narrative
Add text, speech and thoughts
to the pictures; turn parts into a
play script; summarise the story
and tell it; invent and tell other
characters' stories; tell the story
from a different viewpoint

Explanation
Leaflets on immigration: how to
get around, buy food, etc.; the
processing of migrants; how to look
after a 'creature'; why 'creatures'
are important; why do people
migrate?

UNIT PLAN

Theme: *The Arrival* – **Description**   Upper Key Stage 2

FINAL OUTCOME
To write descriptions of the animals (pets) in *The Arrival*

PHASE 1

- Read a range of character/animal descriptions
- Explore and respond – which do you prefer and why?
- Identify audience and purpose for each description read
- Begin to collect writer's hints
- Identify features
- Explore the use of expanded noun phrases; metaphors, onomatopoeia, alliteration to add detail and effect
- Collect and 'play with' effects so that they are internalised and the effects understood
- Chunk a description into sections to get a feel for structure

Phase 1 outcome
To know what good descriptions sound like

PHASE 2

- Play barrier games to support with clarity of descriptions
- Use pictures from *The Arrival* to choose stimulus for writing own description
- Play word and language games to support with finding appropriate noun phrases, metaphors, onomatopoeia and alliteration
- Play games to help imagine the characteristics of each animal (rather than simply physical features)
- Orally rehearse – support with development
- Plan (two different animals)

Phase 2 outcome
To have planned my own descriptions

PHASE 3

- Model how to use plan to write opening of description
- Children write opening independently
- Mark and either model next part or children proceed with writing the rest of their descriptions independently
- Read descriptions aloud in order to support with editing
- Refine, publish and evaluate

UNIT PLAN

Theme: *The Arrival* – Explanation   Upper Key Stage 2

FINAL OUTCOME
Explanation text 'Why
Do People Migrate?'

PHASE 1

- Shared read explanation texts
- Explore and respond, and discuss purpose and audience
- Begin to collect writer's hints
- Immerse the children in explanation texts, including writing and shared reading your own model (e.g. 'Why do animals migrate?')
- Unpick language features and understand why they are used/effective
- Build word bank of technical vocabulary (short write glossary) and other 'explanation'-type words/phrases
- Direct teach around the structure of the explanation text – heading, introduction, paragraph content, conclusion, diagrams/pictures
- Discuss layout (purpose)
- Finalise list of writer's hints

Phase 1 outcome

To know what a good explanation text looks and sounds like

PHASE 2

- Hook: look back at *The Arrival* and discuss why you think that he was leaving his country
- Discuss reasons why people might migrate – do any of the children have relatives who migrated? What are their stories?
- Explain task and begin to build list of technical vocabulary needed
- Play word and language games to practise using 'explanation'-type words/phrases in context
- Plan new text and use drama/role play to explore sections
- Add to plan, including technical vocabulary to be used
- Make decisions about layout: what goes where on the page and why?

Phase 2 outcome

To have planned my explanation text

PHASE 3

- Model write introduction (including focus on vocabulary)
- Children write own
- Shared write first paragraph (including focus on vocabulary)
- Children write own
- Support with decisions about next paragraph, including layout
- Children complete the rest of their explanations
- Mark, feed back and edit (focus on structure and effective vocabulary)
- Publish, share and evaluate

UNIT PLAN

Theme: *The Arrival* – **Narrative**   Upper Key Stage 2

FINAL OUTCOME

To write *The Arrival* as a flashback story

PHASE 1

- Read a range of short stories with flashbacks
- Explore purpose and audience for each
- Explore likes, dislikes, puzzles, patterns for each
- Use mapping to identify typical plot structure to these types of stories, and where the flashback sits (e.g. flashback/opening, build up, problem, resolution, ending *or* opening, build-up, flashback)
- Check that children are clear about how flashback is used to best effect – explore this if necessary using language games
- Collect tools that make a good flashback story – writer's hints
- Collect any language or vocabulary that is effective

Phase 1 outcome

To know what a good flashback story sounds like

PHASE 2

- Hook: read *The Arrival*; task: to tell the story as if you are him telling his grandchildren what happened
- Together map out the key events
- Use drama and role-play to guide thinking through (1) main events and (2) how characters might feel and react (description/action/dialogue to portray this)
- Decide on best moment to flashback
- Create individual story maps showing the main events and flashback – shape into a plan
- Use drama to add to ideas around action/dialogue; add to story maps
- Orally rehearse use of collected language
- Finalise plan

Phase 2 outcome

To have planned my flashback story

PHASE 3

- Briefly remind children of expectations and check that all are ready to write
- Children independently write the first two sections of the story
- Mark and follow up on issues before they move onto the next parts
- Shared write to support, where necessary – especially the flashback part
- Children independently write rest of story
- Support them to edit and refine story
- Publish, share and evaluate

Poetry
Witches; forests; seasons; fire; fantasy settings; lists; story poems (happy endings)

Description
Collect the imagery and use to write new descriptions; describe: the witch; Jub; Jub's home; the wildlife; the old oak tree; contrasting settings children's homes with forest or witch's house

The Lost Happy Endings
by Carol Ann Duffy and Jane Ray

Narrative
Write another golden pen story; write the story from the witch's point of view; write a new 'witch's story' (from the middle of the book); write a new ending for one of the stories that lost its ending

Instructions
How to rescue the lost happy endings; how to climb trees; directions – how to find a golden pen, routes through the forest; recipes – happy endings; witch's spells

UNIT PLAN

Theme: *The Lost Happy Endings* – Setting descriptions   Lower Key Stage 2

FINAL OUTCOME
To write two contrasting setting descriptions

PHASE 1

- Shared read known stories and use them to discuss what 'settings' are
- Shared read variety of good-quality setting descriptions
- Collect writer's hints
- Play word/language games to develop the language of description
- Chunk a setting description into parts so that children understand structure
- Hook – read *The Lost Happy Endings* and respond (likes/dislikes/puzzles/patterns)
- Focus on the settings (forest, Jub's house, witch's house) and collect vocabulary from the book

Phase 1 outcome

To know what a good setting description sounds like

PHASE 2

- Begin with Jub's house – use pictures from the book and other pictures/artefacts to build a picture of the setting
- Label with vocabulary; build a bank
- Support the children to create a plan for the setting description
- Pair work – children 'talk' their descriptions (use collected vocabulary and similes effectively)
- Play word/language games to continue to develop and rehearse the language of description
- Carry out the same process as above but for the witch's house – make sure the settings are contrasting

Phase 2 outcome

To have planned my two setting descriptions

PHASE 3

- For Jub's house: model write first couple of lines (including modelling how to work from a plan)
- Children independently write their descriptions
- Share and refine
- Children independently write their descriptions of the witch's house (putting into practice what they have learned from Jub's house descriptions)
- Edit, refine and publish

UNIT PLAN

Theme: *The Lost Happy Endings* – Instructions   Lower Key Stage 2

FINAL OUTCOME
To write a recipe for a witch's spell

PHASE 1

- Hook – read *The Lost Happy Endings*
- Explain task – to write a recipe that might be found in the witch's spell book
- Shared read various recipes (real and fictional)
- Explore and respond – compare and contrast
- Identify the features and typical language of recipes (e.g. introduction, what you need, what you do, bossy verbs, ordered steps, concluding statement)
- Collect writer's hints for recipes
- Play language games to develop understanding of bossy verb meanings (e.g. mime the action)
- Chunk text into sections and discuss layout (purpose)

Phase 1 outcome
To know what a good recipe looks and sounds like

PHASE 2

- Read more witch's spells to support children with generating ideas
- Use talk activities to explore what the witch's spell is going to be for, and therefore what ingredients she might need
- Agree what the spell is for
- Use chunks from phase 1 to begin to plan new recipe
- Talk activities to support with ideas for what you might put into an introduction, and the 'what you need' section
- Talk activities to support with ideas for adding detail into each step (e.g. when you push the button, wait, hold your breath for ten seconds)
- Support with ideas for a concluding statement
- Complete plan

Phase 2 outcome
To have planned my recipe

PHASE 3

- Shared write introduction
- Children write introduction and 'what you need' independently
- Shared write initial steps
- Children write steps independently
- Shared write concluding statement
- Children complete independently
- Mark, feed back and edit
- Publish and share

UNIT PLAN

Theme: *The Lost Happy Endings* – **Narrative**   Lower Key Stage 2

FINAL OUTCOME
To write the witch's story of *The Lost Happy Endings*

PHASE 1

- Read *The Lost Happy Endings* and respond (likes, dislikes, puzzles, patterns)
- Map the story (use a mountain if necessary)
- Familiarise the children with the plot so that they can retell it in summary form
- Shared read stories from different viewpoints (e.g. *The True Story of the 3 Little Pigs*; *Seriously, Cinderella Is So Annoying*)
- Explore and respond – likes, dislikes, puzzles, patterns
- Collect list of writer's hints for these stories

Phase 1 outcome

To know *The Lost Happy Endings* story and what a good story from an alternative viewpoint sounds like

PHASE 2

- Use drama/freeze-framing to explore the plot from the point of view of the witch
- Create a new map or storyboard of the main events
- Hot-seat the witch to discover how she feels about Jub, stories with happy endings; and what she did and why
- Add to map or storyboard, then transfer to a plan
- Use word/language games to explore new vocabulary
- Orally rehearse new ideas
- Finalise plan

Phase 2 outcome

To have planned my story

PHASE 3

- Show children mock-up of final book
- Model write opening – using story map/board/plan
- Children write opening independently
- Model write main events – using story map/board/plan
- Children write main events independently
- Model write ending – using story map/board/plan
- Children write ending independently
- Mark, feed back and edit
- Publish and share

Recount
Newspaper reports about the events; magazine article about the flying frog phenomenon; email from male character; police report; eyewitness reports

Description
Scenes from the flight of the frogs; frog study; home/garden settings; character descriptions

Tuesday
by David Wiesner

Narrative
Write the story of the book; write the sequel (pigs); write a prequel; write the story from a character's point of view; write the story as a flashback or with a cliffhanger ending

Explanation
Wikipedia page on 'why the frogs were flying' or 'how do lily-pads fly?'; frog life cycles; investigator's explanation of the events

UNIT PLAN

Theme: *Tuesday* – Explanation   Lower Key Stage 2

FINAL OUTCOME

To write an explanation of the *Life Cycle of a Frog*

PHASE 1

- Play talk games to establish what an explanation is (e.g. explain how you got to school this morning, explain why the sky is blue)
- Shared read explanation texts
- Explore and respond – likes, dislikes, puzzles, patterns; and identify audience and purpose of each
- Immerse children in explanation texts so that they know the typical language patterns
- Unpick language features and add key ones to writer's hints
- Collect effective vocabulary/language of explanations
- Chunk text and identify layout features (e.g. diagrams, bullets, headings and purpose of each feature)

Phase 1 outcome

To know what a good explanation looks and sounds like

PHASE 2

- Hook children in to the topic of *Life Cycle of a Frog*
- Using pictures as a stimulus play talk games to explain each part of the life cycle
- Introduce new technical vocabulary and play talk games for children to orally rehearse
- Use text chunked in phase 1 to help plan new explanation
- Play word/language games to orally rehearse the life cycle together with the language of explanation
- Finalise plan

Phase 2 outcome

To have planned my explanation

PHASE 3

- Show children a mock-up of final explanation (i.e. how it could be laid out on the page)
- Shared write opening of explanation – model how to use plan
- Children independently write the opening
- Mark and follow up on issues before they move onto the main body of the explanation
- Shared write to support with main body and closing
- Children independently write rest of explanation
- Add additional elements (e.g. headings, diagrams)
- Support them to edit and refine whole text
- Publish, share and evaluate

UNIT PLAN

Theme: *Tuesday* – Narrative

Lower Key Stage 2

FINAL OUTCOME

To write a sequel to *Tuesday*

PHASE 1

- Read *Tuesday* and respond (likes, dislikes, puzzles, patterns)
- Write a simple model of the story of *Tuesday*, map it and support children to be able to retell it
- Shared read stories with similar plot patterns
- Explore and respond – likes, dislikes, puzzles, patterns
- Collect effective vocabulary and language and create list of writer's hints
- Chunk the model into sections – use drama/role play to understand key parts of the story

Phase 1 outcome

To know the *Tuesday* story and what makes a good story of this type

PHASE 2

- Reread *Tuesday* and pay close attention to the final illustration (pigs flying)
- Use picture stimulus to discuss other adventures that could be had – who might the pigs see and where might they go?
- Use drama/role play to explore new adventures
- Collect vocabulary along the way
- Create new plan
- Use word/language games to explore new vocabulary
- Orally rehearse new ideas
- Finalise plan

Phase 2 outcome

To have planned my sequel to *Tuesday*

PHASE 3

- Show children mock-up of final book
- Model write opening – using plan
- Children write opening independently
- Model write main events – using plan
- Children write main events independently
- Model write ending – using plan
- Children write ending independently
- Mark, feed back and edit
- Publish, share and evaluate

UNIT PLAN

Theme: *Tuesday* – **Newspaper reports**   Lower Key Stage 2

FINAL OUTCOME
Newspaper report on the events of *Tuesday*

PHASE 1

- Hook – watch *Guardian* newspaper advert (3 Little Pigs)
- General discussion re: newspaper reports – purpose and audience
- Shared read age-appropriate newspaper reports and respond
- Immerse children in newspaper reports so that they internalise the language patterns
- Discuss how stories are handled/portrayed
- Check understanding of purpose and audience of newspaper reports
- Collect list of writer's hints, and appropriate vocabulary
- Chunk newspaper report into sections to check understanding of typical structure

Phase 1 outcome
To know what a good newspaper report looks and sounds like

PHASE 2

- Read *Tuesday*
- Explore key events through drama/freeze-framing and hot-seating
- Use chunks from phase 1 to plan/structure new ideas
- Explore headline to use
- Orally rehearse, using language collected in phase 1; add ideas to plan
- Finalise plan

Phase 2 outcome
To have planned my newspaper report

PHASE 3

- Shared write opening, including headline and use of language
- Children independently write openings
- Shared write next parts picking up on issues as report progresses
- Children independently write next parts
- Peer evaluate success, then edit
- Publish

Recount
Eyewitness reports
(dog goes missing); diary entries;
individual recounts of events
at the park (viewpoint);
autobiographies

Description
Characters; the park at different
moments in the book; thoughts
and feelings of characters
at key moments

Voices in the Park
by Anthony Browne

Narrative
Tell the story; write it as a
play script; write a new adventure
for one of the characters;
write the sequel

Persuasion
Letters: application from 'dad'
(for a job); persuading 'mum' to
be nice to Charles; from 'dad'
to 'mum' asking her to let
Smudge play with Charles
again

UNIT PLAN

Theme: *Voices in the Park* – Recount (biography)   Key Stage 2

FINAL OUTCOME

To write a biography based on *Voices in the Park*

PHASE 1

- Shared read biographies from Marcia Williams's *Three Cheers for Inventors*
- Respond – likes, dislikes, puzzles, patterns; and identify purpose and audience
- General discussion re: biographies – check children understand the purpose and audience
- Immerse the children in short biographies
- Identify use of language, collect and create list of writer's hints
- Chunk a simple biography into sections (opening, childhood paragraph(s), later life paragraph(s), conclusion) so that children understand structure

Phase 1 outcome

To know what a good biography sounds like

PHASE 2

- Hook – read *Voices in the Park*
- Hot-seat 'mum' or 'dad' (and others, e.g. Smudge, Charles) to find out about his or her life
- Use talk activities to decide on extra detail; perhaps they experienced something traumatic, maybe a relative was famous, etc.
- Use chunks from phase 1 to plan biography
- Orally rehearse use of effective language (collected in phase 1)
- Add to plan

Phase 2 outcome

To have planned my biography

PHASE 3

- Shared write opening
- Independent and guided write openings
- Shared write next parts picking up on issues as biography progresses
- Support with concluding paragraph – check it has impact
- Check that the biography has a sensible chronological order and is interesting to read
- Edit and evaluate
- Publish

UNIT PLAN

Theme: *Voices in the Park* – Persuasion

Key Stage 2

FINAL OUTCOME

Persuasive letter based on *Voices in the Park*

PHASE 1

- Hook: Read *Voices in the Park* and read letter from Charles to Smudge asking whether she could meet in the park again
- Explain task – dad writing a letter to mum to persuade her to let Charles and Smudge meet again
- General discussion 'what is persuasion?' Talk activities to support children with understanding persuasion
- Shared read a variety of persuasive letters
- Discuss purpose and audience; compare and contrast – which work best and why?
- Identify use of language, collect effective language and vocabulary
- Build list of writer's hints for letters of persuasion
- Chunk a persuasive letter into sections
- Recap understanding of layout of letters

Phase 1 outcome

To know what a good persuasive letter looks and sounds like

PHASE 2

- Use drama/role play to explore the arguments that dad would make; collect ideas
- Group ideas into themes and generate persuasive sentences – orally rehearse to check that they sound right and have the right effect
- Check children are clear about purpose and audience for letter
- Use chunks from phase 1 to plan new letter
- Take elements from the list of hints and practise using them as part of the arguments
- Orally rehearse each section of the letter
- Add vocabulary to plan

Phase 2 outcome

To have planned my persuasive letter

PHASE 3

- Shared write opening of letter – model how to use plan
- Children independently write the opening
- Mark and follow up on issues before they move onto the main body of the letter
- Shared write to support with main body and closing
- Children independently write rest of letter
- Support them to edit and refine whole text
- Publish, share and evaluate
- Send letters to mum and see if she replies!

UNIT PLAN

Theme: *Voices in the Park* – Play script

Key Stage 2

FINAL OUTCOME

To write a play script of *Voices in the Park*

PHASE 1

- Read *Voices in the Park* and respond: likes, dislikes, puzzles, patterns
- Go through each voice and analyse – use the illustrations to discuss character and relationships
- Explore purpose and audience; why do you think Anthony Browne wrote this and what is his message?
- Read short plays and analyse for the conventions
- Compare and contrast (look for which are more effectively written and why)
- Collect effective vocabulary from narrations/stage directions
- Collect writer's hints for play scripts

Phase 1 outcome

To know *Voices in the Park* and the features of play scripts

PHASE 2

- Focus on first voice: use drama to act out
- Freeze-frame key moments and discuss how to record as a play script
- Collect vocabulary for narrations/stage directions
- Storyboard first voice (as plan)
- Children choose a second voice to focus on – repeat the process of drama and storyboarding to collect ideas and plan
- More voices can be covered if required

Phase 2 outcome

To have planned my play script

PHASE 3

- Shared write play script opening for first voice
- Children independently write first voice play script
- Support with editing and refining discussions
- Repeat process for second voice
- Perform, share and evaluate

Recount
Newspaper reports about child homelessness or about Shane; diary entries; Shane's journal; letters from Shane; biography

Description
Scenes from the streets; the cat; Shane; Shane's home; contrasts within the book – dark/light; describe a new home for Shane

Way Home
by Libby Hathorn and Gregory Rogers

Narrative
Rewrite the story change the main character or the ending or the chronology; turn key moments into play scripts; write from a different point of view; write a new story for Shane

Persuasion
Homelessness/child homelessness: leaflets; magazine articles; flyers; campaign letters; letters from Shane's family; letters to MPs

UNIT PLAN

Theme: *Way Home* – Narrative

Upper Key Stage 2

FINAL OUTCOME

To write a new story for Shane in the style of *Way Home*

PHASE 1

- Read *Way Home* and respond (likes, dislikes, puzzles, patterns)
- Map story to show plot structure
- Act out and freeze frame key moments from the story – play with the order of events, sequence the events – which is better and why?
- Focus on how key moments are portrayed by the author/illustrator – discuss what makes them effective
- Discuss how suspense is built
- Collect writer's hints
- Collect any language or vocabulary that is effective

Phase 1 outcome

To know *Way Home* and what makes it a good story

PHASE 2

- Task: think of another event for Shane that would make a good story
- Try out ideas by acting them out
- Decide on plot line and use drama and role play to help with (1) adding description and detail and (2) building suspense
- Begin to develop new plan
- Use oral rehearsal and language games to add ideas and tweak plan
- Orally rehearse use of collected language
- Finalise plan

Phase 2 outcome

To have planned my Shane story

PHASE 3

- Briefly remind children of expectations and check that all are ready to write
- Children independently write the first two sections of the story
- Mark and follow up on issues before they move onto the next parts
- Shared write to support, where necessary – especially the use of suspense
- Children independently write rest of story
- Support them to edit and refine story
- Publish, share and evaluate

UNIT PLAN

Theme: *Way Home* – Newspaper reports   Upper Key Stage 2

FINAL OUTCOME

Newspaper report on homelessness based on *Way Home*

PHASE 1

- Read *Way Home* and respond
- Discuss what children know and understand about homelessness
- Explain that newspaper reports are often about important social issues
- Shared read a selection of issue-based newspaper reports (can watch TV news reports too)
- Discuss the audience and purpose
- Identify use of journalistic language, collect and check understanding
- Collect list of writer's hints for newspaper reports
- Chunk newspaper report into sections to check understanding of typical structure
- Recap understanding of layout of newspaper reports

Phase 1 outcome

To know what a good newspaper report looks and sounds like

PHASE 2

- Use pictures and facts/figures to show children the reality of homelessness in their local area
- Use talk activities to explore the key areas that might be covered in a newspaper report about homelessness
- Begin to plan – grouping themes and adding detail
- Orally rehearse effective vocabulary, and add to plan
- Explore headline to use
- Orally rehearse use of journalistic language
- Research facts/figures to add weight to report
- Finalise plan

Phase 2 outcome

To have planned my newspaper report

PHASE 3

- Shared write opening, including headline and use of language
- Children independently write openings
- Shared write next parts picking up on issues as report progresses
- Children independently write next parts
- Peer evaluate success, then edit
- Publish

UNIT PLAN

Theme: *Way Home* – Persuasion   Upper Key Stage 2

FINAL OUTCOME
Persuasive letter
based on *Way Home*

PHASE 1

- Hook – read *Way Home* and respond
- Discuss what children know and understand about homelessness
- Explain that if you feel strongly about an issue you can campaign; discuss letter writing as a campaign method
- Shared read a variety of persuasive letters (some too aggressive, unclear etc.), including an 'issue'-based letter
- Discuss purpose and audience; compare and contrast – which work best and why?
- Identify use of language, collect and check understanding of what makes it effective
- Collect list of writer's hints for letters of persuasion
- Chunk a persuasive letter into sections

Phase 1 outcome

To know what a good persuasive letter looks and sounds like

PHASE 2

- Use pictures and facts/figures to show children the reality of homelessness in their local area
- Use drama/role play to explore the arguments that you might put to an MP regarding homelessness
- Group ideas into themes and generate persuasive sentences – orally rehearse to check that they sound right and have the right effect
- Use chunks from phase 1 to plan new letter
- Add vocabulary to plan

Phase 2 outcome

To have planned my persuasive letter

PHASE 3

- Shared write opening of letter – model how to use plan
- Children independently write the opening
- Mark and follow up on issues before they move onto the main body of the letter
- Shared write to support with main body and closing
- Children independently write rest of letter
- Support them to edit and refine whole text
- Publish, share and evaluate
- Send letters to an MP and see if he or she replies!

Explanation
How unusual fruits/veg grow;
how to spin a robe from the fibres
of stalks telling the time from a sundial;
Wes's counting system or sports;
glossary of Wes's language

Description
Settings for a travel
brochure; unusual fruits and
veg; characters

Weslandia
by Paul
Fleischman

Narrative
The schoolmate's story; sequel;
flashback story; change the detail
of Weslandia (i.e. the middle
of the story)

Persuasion
For or against living in
Weslandia; adverts: travel
writing (visit Weslandia)
or Wes's oil

Recount
How Wes created Weslandia;
different viewpoints on the key
events; newspaper/broadcast
reports; extracts from
Wes's diary

UNIT PLAN

Theme: *Weslandia* – Setting description

Upper Key Stage 2

FINAL OUTCOME
To write setting description of *Weslandia* for a travel brochure

PHASE 1

- Read a range of setting descriptions (including travel brochure descriptions)
- Explore and respond – which do you prefer and why?
- Identify audience and purpose for each description read
- Begin to collect writer's hints
- Identify features of persuasive descriptions
- Explore the use of expanded noun phrases, metaphors, onomatopoeia, alliteration to add detail and effect
- Collect and 'play with' effects found in travel brochures
- Chunk a typical brochure description to get a feel for structure

Phase 1 outcome
To know what good setting descriptions/ travel brochure pieces sound like

PHASE 2

- Play barrier games to support with clarity of descriptions
- Use pictures from *Weslandia* to choose stimulus for writing own description
- Begin to plan, using chunks from phase 1
- Play word and language games to support with finding appropriate noun phrases, metaphors, onomatopoeia and alliteration to describe settings
- Orally rehearse – support with development
- Finalise plan (bear in mind audience and purpose)

Phase 2 outcome
To have planned my own setting description

PHASE 3

- Model how to use plan to write opening of setting description
- Children write opening independently
- Mark and either model next part or children proceed with writing the rest of their descriptions independently
- Read descriptions aloud in order to support with editing
- Evaluate
- Refine and publish

UNIT PLAN

Theme: *Weslandia* – Discussion   Upper Key Stage 2

FINAL OUTCOME
To write a discussion about whether Weslandia is a good place to live

PHASE 1

- Read a range of discussion texts (factual rather than persuasive and emotive)
- Explore purpose and audience for each; agree basic principles of these kinds of discussions
- Use talk activities to further explore the concept of 'discussion'
- Collect list of writer's hints
- Play language games to practise using discursive language
- Chunk a discursive text into sections to clarify structure of discussion texts (paragraphs: intro, points for, points against, conclusion)

Phase 1 outcome
To know what good discussion texts look and sound like

PHASE 2

- Reread *Weslandia* – hook into discussion title: 'Is Weslandia a good place to live?'
- Use chunks from phase 1 to start to plan new discussion
- Use discussion-based role-play and drama games to explore ideas for and against living in Weslandia
- Use language games to further explore the effective use of discursive language
- Orally rehearse possible introductions/conclusions to this discussion
- Complete plan

Phase 2 outcome
To have planned my own discussion text

PHASE 3

- Shared write introduction and points for paragraph(s)
- Children independently write introduction and points for paragraph(s)
- Shared write points against and concluding paragraphs
- Children independently write points against and concluding paragraphs
- Support with editing and refining discussions
- Share and evaluate

UNIT PLAN

Theme: *Weslandia – Narrative*   Upper Key Stage 2

FINAL OUTCOME
To write a good versus evil story set in Weslandia, with Wesley as the hero

PHASE 1

- Read a range of short stories with good versus evil as the underlying theme
- Respond and explore purpose and audience for each
- Collect good versus evil vocabulary
- Use mapping or a story mountain to identify typical plot structure to these types of stories (i.e. opening, build-up, problem, etc.
- Check that children are clear about 'suspense', which is usually used in the build-up and problem parts
- Collect hints – tools that make a good versus evil story effective

Phase 1 outcome

To know what a good versus evil story sounds like

PHASE 2

- Hook: reread Weslandia. Set up scene that Weslandia is attacked, support children to think about who might have attacked it and why?
- Use drama and role play to guide thinking through (1) main events, (2) Wes's feelings and reactions (description/action/dialogue), (3) Resolution events NB Remember suspense
- Create individual story maps/mountains showing the main events (problem) and how they were solved (resolution)
- Use talk activities to think through the build-up (suspense) and ending to the narrative; add to story maps
- Orally rehearse using collected hints and vocabulary
- Finalise plan

Phase 2 outcome

To have planned my good versus evil story

PHASE 3

- Briefly remind children of expectations and check that all are ready to write
- Children independently write the opening and build-up paragraphs
- Mark and follow up on issues before they move onto the problem and resolution parts
- Shared write to support, where necessary
- Children independently write rest of story
- Support them to edit and refine story
- Share and evaluate

CHAPTER 2

Using novels and
short stories as hooks

Mind maps
and unit plans

Instructions
How to survive in a dress; how to be a boy or girl for the day; how to be [someone or something else] for the day; rules for being inclusive

Description
Characters: Bill as a girl and as a boy, Mean Malcolm, Mrs Collins; setting: school

Bill's New Frock
by Anne Fine

Narrative
Write your own change story; write an alternative version with a girl as the main character; add a new character who knows what's going on; change the ending

Discussion
Are some jobs right for men and some for women? Should Bill tell someone what's happened to him? Does Bill enjoy wearing a frock? Is our school playground inclusive?

UNIT PLAN

<u>Theme</u>: *Bill's New Frock* – Discussion   Year 2/Lower Key Stage 2

PHASE 1

- Shared read a range of age-appropriate discussion texts
- Use talk activities to further explore the concept of 'discussion'
- Immerse children in simple discussion texts
- Check understanding of typical language/vocabulary
- Play language games to practise using simple discursive language and understand what makes it effective
- Collect list of writer's hints
- Chunk simple text into sections and discuss layout (purpose)
- Clarify structure of discussion texts (paragraphs: intro, points for, points against, conclusion) NB This is easier for children if the title is expressed as a question, e.g. Do all girls have to wear dresses?

FINAL OUTCOME

To write a discussion about whether Bill enjoyed wearing the frock

Phase 1 outcome

To know what a good discussion text looks and sounds like

PHASE 2

- Hook – read extracts from *Bill's New Frock* and collect reasons for/against him liking wearing the frock
- Introduce task and hold an initial class discussion on this (count numbers for/against as baseline)
- Use discussion-based role-play and drama games (e.g. conscience alley) to explore reasons for and against him liking wearing the frock
- Start to plan discussion
- Use language games to further explore the effective use of discursive language, and other aspects on the hints list
- Orally rehearse possible introductions/conclusions to this discussion
- Complete plan

Phase 2 outcome

To have planned my own discussion text

PHASE 3

- Shared write introduction and points for paragraph
- Children independently write introduction and points for paragraph
- Shared write points against and concluding paragraphs
- Children independently write points against and concluding paragraphs
- Support with editing and refining discussions
- Share and evaluate
- Publish
- Hold second count to see if anyone changed their mind!

UNIT PLAN

Theme: *Bill's New Frock* – Instructions   Year 2/Lower Key Stage 2

FINAL OUTCOME
To write a set of instructions

PHASE 1

- Hook – extracts from *Bill's New Frock*
- Explain task – to write a set of instructions for how to be something or someone else for the day
- Shared read various sets of instructions
- Explore and respond – compare and contrast
- Identify the features and typical language of instructions (e.g. introduction, what you need, what you do, bossy verbs, ordered steps, concluding statement)
- Build list of writer's hints for instructions
- Play language games to develop understanding of bossy verb meanings (e.g. mime the action)
- Chunk text into sections and discuss layout (purpose)

Phase 1 outcome

To know what a good set of instructions looks and sounds like

PHASE 2

- Use drama/role play to explore the instructions you might give for being someone or something else for the day
- Use chunks from phase 1 to begin to plan new set
- Practise use of bossy verbs appropriate to this set of instructions
- Talk activities to support with ideas for what you might put into an introduction, and the 'what you need' section
- Talk activities to support with ideas for adding detail into each step (e.g. make sure that you know what games you will play at playtime)
- Support with ideas for a concluding statement
- Complete plan

Phase 2 outcome

To have planned my instructions

PHASE 3

- Shared write introduction
- Children write introduction and 'what you need' independently
- Shared write initial steps
- Children write steps independently
- Shared write concluding statement
- Children complete independently
- Mark, feed back and edit
- Publish and share

UNIT PLAN

Theme: *Bill's New Frock* – Narrative

Year 2/Lower Key Stage 2

FINAL OUTCOME

To write a change story based on *Bill's New Frock*

PHASE 1

- Read *Bill's New Frock* and respond
- Discuss and collect other examples of stories where someone or something has changed
- Shared read and collect plot patterns
- Begin to collect writer's hints for these stories
- Write a brief summarised version – 250–300 words – of *Bill's New Frock* (ensure that writer's hints are woven through the model text) and shared read
- Use a story map to plot events visually – use drama/role play to understand key parts of the plot, especially how the change affected him
- Collect narrative language and effective vocabulary

Phase 1 outcome

To know the plot and narrative language in *Bill's New Frock* and be able to retell it in summary

PHASE 2

- Use picture stimulus to discuss other changes that could happen to someone or something (similar to Bill)
- Use drama/role play to explore new change – what would happen and how does the change affect him/her/it?
- Collect vocabulary along the way
- Use plot structure identified in phase 1 to begin to plan
- Use word/language games to explore new vocabulary
- Orally rehearse new ideas
- Finalise plan

Phase 2 outcome

To have planned my own change story

PHASE 3

- Show children mock-up of final book
- Model write opening – using plan
- Children write opening independently
- Model write main events – using plan
- Children write main events independently
- Model write ending – using plan
- Children write ending independently
- Mark, feed back and edit
- Publish and share

Persuasion
Letter to persuade: Willy Wonka to have you as the sixth guest; your head teacher to let you visit a sweet factory; Charlie to take you instead of grandpa; argument: Charlie is not the best guest; adverts: for the factory; a new sweet; jobs at the factory

Description
Settings: new room in the factory; characters: new golden ticket winner/parent; new Oompa Loompas

Charlie and the Chocolate Factory
by Roald Dahl

Narrative
Write a new chapter for a new room in the factory with a new character getting 'lost' in it; new scene where new character wins golden ticket; Oompa Loompa play script

Instructions
Recipes for Willy Wonka sweets; new sweet recipes; how to win a golden ticket; how to find your way around Willy Wonka's factory; how to care for an Oompa Loompa; factory rules poster/ instruction leaflet for guests

UNIT PLAN

Theme: *Charlie and the Chocolate Factory* – Setting descriptions

Year 2/Lower Key Stage 2

FINAL OUTCOME
To write two setting descriptions

PHASE 1

- Shared read known stories and use them to discuss what 'settings' are
- Shared read and immerse children in a variety of good-quality setting descriptions
- Collect list of writer's hints for setting descriptions
- Play word/language games to develop the language of description
- Chunk a setting description into parts so that children understand structure
- Hook – read Roald Dahl setting descriptions, including rooms in the factory and respond (likes/dislikes/puzzles/patterns)
- Collect any useful vocabulary

Phase 1 outcome
To know what a good setting description sounds like

PHASE 2

- Begin with one of the descriptions of a room in the factory – use talk games to build a picture of the setting
- Label with vocabulary; build a bank
- Support the children to create a plan for the setting description
- Introduce stimulus for new room in the factory (e.g. marshmallow room); use senses to build a description of the room
- Play word/language games to continue to develop ideas for what the room would look/feel like
- Create a plan for the new room
- Support children to 'talk' their descriptions to orally rehearse and refine them
- Finalise second plan

Phase 2 outcome
To have planned my two setting descriptions

PHASE 3

- For first setting: model write first couple of lines (including modelling how to work from a plan)
- Children independently write their descriptions
- Share and refine
- Children independently write their descriptions of the new room (putting into practice what they have learned from first setting descriptions)
- Edit, refine and publish

UNIT PLAN

Theme: *Charlie and the Chocolate Factory* – **Narrative**   Year 2/Lower Key Stage 2

FINAL OUTCOME

To write a new chapter for *Charlie and the Chocolate Factory* (involves new character in a new room)

PHASE 1

- Hook – use clips of key moments from Roald Dahl films
- General discussion re: Roald Dahl's work similarities/differences/likes/dislikes
- Read extracts from *Charlie, Danny, Matilda* – compare plot and characters
- Read and plot visually (map or story mountain) chapter from *Charlie* in which a child gets 'lost' in a room: identify plot pattern
- Collect effective language and vocabulary
- Collect list of writer's hints

Phase 1 outcome

To know Dahl's style of plot and how language is used for effect

PHASE 2

- Use clips from the film of *Charlie and the Chocolate Factory* to study the rooms and events (previously decided character/room should be used here)
- Drama and storyboarding to decide on new event in new room
- Focus on use of language – description, action, dialogue
- Orally rehearse; record key ideas
- Complete plan using mapped chapter as a model structure

Phase 2 outcome

To have planned my new chapter

PHASE 3

- Model write opening – using plan
- Children write opening independently
- Model write main events – using plan
- Children write main events independently
- Model write ending – using plan
- Children write ending independently
- Mark, feedback and edit
- Publish and share

UNIT PLAN

Theme: *Charlie and the Chocolate Factory* – Persuasion   Year 2/Lower Key Stage 2

FINAL OUTCOME
Persuasive letter based on *Charlie and the Chocolate Factory*

PHASE 1

- Hook – read a made-up letter to Willy Wonka persuading him to let you be the sixth guest
- Shared read a variety of persuasive letters (some too aggressive, unclear, etc.)
- Discuss purpose and audience; compare and contrast – which work best and why?
- Identify use of language, collect effective language and vocabulary
- Build list of writer's hints for letters of persuasion
- Chunk a persuasive letter into sections
- Teach or recap layout of letters

Phase 1 outcome
To know what a good persuasive letter looks and sounds like

PHASE 2

- Introduce task: to persuade Charlie to take you instead of Grandpa Joe
- Use drama/role play to explore the arguments that you might put to him
- Group ideas and generate persuasive sentences – orally rehearse to check that they sound right and have the right effect
- Check children are clear about purpose and audience for letter
- Use chunks from phase 1 to plan new letter
- Take elements from the writer's hints and practise using them as part of the arguments
- Orally rehearse each section of the letter
- Add vocabulary to plan

Phase 2 outcome
To have planned my persuasive letter

PHASE 3

- Shared write opening of letter – model how to use plan
- Children independently write the opening
- Mark and follow up on issues before they move onto the main body of the letter
- Shared write to support with main body and closing
- Children independently write rest of letter
- Support them to edit and refine whole text
- Publish, share and evaluate
- Send letters to Charlie and see if he replies!

Recount
Diary entries; letters; postcards;
coming to England journey recounts;
family biographies

Description
Cooking-related recount/
descriptions; characters: Grandpa
Chatterji; Grandpa Leicester;
Neetu; Sanjay; settings:
home; fairground; poppy
field

Grandpa Chatterji
by
Jamila Gavin

Narrative
Write a new chapter
(e.g. Chatterji takes Leicester
shopping); add more rides to
'Grandpa rides in a rocket'
chapter; rewrite a chapter from
Grandpa's viewpoint

Instructions
How to make Grandpa
Chatterji/Leicester feel welcome;
how to cook; house rules;
flower pressing; how to ride
in a rocket

UNIT PLAN

Theme: *Grandpa Chatterji* – **Instructions**   Year 2/Lower Key Stage 2

FINAL OUTCOME
To write a set of instructions

PHASE 1

- Hook – fairground ride photographs and video clips
- Explain task – to write a set of instructions for how to ride in a rocket (linked to the chapter in *Grandpa Chatterji*); invent audience
- Shared read various sets of instructions
- Explore and respond – compare and contrast
- Identify the features and typical language of instructions (e.g. introduction, what you need, what you do, bossy verbs, ordered steps, concluding statement)
- Build list of writer's hints for instructions
- Play language games to develop understanding of bossy verb meanings (e.g. mime the action)
- Chunk text into sections and discuss layout (purpose)

Phase 1 outcome

To know what a good set of instructions looks and sounds like

PHASE 2

- Reread extracts from the chapter and use drama/role play to explore the instructions you might give for riding on the different fairground rides
- Use chunks from phase 1 to begin to plan new set
- Practise use of bossy verbs appropriate to this set of instructions
- Talk activities to support with ideas for what you might put into an introduction, and the 'what you need' section
- Talk activities to support with ideas for adding detail into each step (e.g. make sure that you are properly strapped into your seat)
- Support with ideas for a concluding statement
- Complete plan

Phase 2 outcome

To have planned my instructions

PHASE 3

- Shared write introduction
- Children write introduction and 'what you need' independently
- Shared write initial steps
- Children write steps independently
- Shared write concluding statement
- Children complete independently
- Mark, feed back and edit
- Publish and share

UNIT PLAN

Theme: *Grandpa Chatterji* – **Narrative**   Lower Key Stage 2/Year 2

FINAL OUTCOME

To write 'Grandpa rides in a rocket' from his viewpoint

PHASE 1

- Read the chapter from *Grandpa Chatterji*
- Respond and discuss – likes/dislikes/puzzles/patterns
- Begin to collect writer's hints by discussing what Jamila Gavin did to make the chapter engaging and effective
- Use mapping to identify key events of the chapter – use drama/role play to understand them
- Collect effective vocabulary and language
- Shared read the first part of the chapter and start to consider how it would be effectively turned into a first-person narrative – it would probably start with Grandpa reminiscing about fairs in India

Phase 1 outcome

To know the plot and narrative language in the chosen chapter

PHASE 2

- Use the mapping activity from phase 1 to support the children to convert the main events into a first-person narrative
- Collect vocabulary along the way
- Hot-seat Grandpa to find out more
- Annotate the plan or map as the chapter progresses
- Use word/language games to explore new vocabulary
- Orally rehearse new ideas
- Use talk activities to support with planning how the chapter will end
- Finalise plan

Phase 2 outcome

To have planned my new chapter

PHASE 3

- Model write opening – using plan
- Children write opening independently
- Model write main events – using plan
- Children write main events independently
- Model write ending – using plan
- Children write ending independently
- Mark, feed back and edit
- Publish and share

UNIT PLAN

Theme: *Grandpa Chatterji* – Recount (diary)   Year 2/Lower Key Stage 2

FINAL OUTCOME

To write Grandpa Leicester's recount of his visit, as a diary entry

PHASE 1

- Hook – read 'When Grandpa Leicester came to stay' chapter and discuss – did he enjoy his visit and why?
- Introduce task
- Shared read diary entries and respond (likes/dislikes/puzzles/patterns)
- Compare and contrast: which is better and why?
- Write a model diary entry that Neetu might have written recounting Grandpa's visit; shared read and familiarise the children with the language patterns and vocabulary
- Use a map to chunk the story into key events – build a bank of vocabulary for each, and develop children's understanding of this vocabulary
- Use the model to support knowledge of structure and explore the use of time connectives
- Collect writer's hints for diary entries

Phase 1 outcome

To know what a good recount looks and sounds like

PHASE 2

- If necessary, use the map of events to support the children to role-play (and understand) the main events in the chapter
- Use freeze-framing to support the children to think about how Grandpa Leicester felt at each point
- Hot-seat Grandpa Leicester
- Collect vocabulary
- Support children to complete their plan
- Play word/language games to orally rehearse the use of time words – children add these to their plan

Phase 2 outcome

To have planned my recount

PHASE 3

- Shared write opening of diary entry (recount) – model how to use plan
- Children independently write the opening
- Mark and follow up on issues before they move onto the main body of the recount
- Shared write to support with main body and closing
- Children independently write rest of recount
- Support them to edit and refine whole text
- Publish, share and evaluate

Information
Reports on: reptiles, animals with shells, natural camouflage and protection; wiki page on how the tortoise got his crooked shell (or similar)

Description
Write descriptions of animals' skins, shells, features; describe animals' movement (flight, running, walking, etc.)

How the Tortoise Got His Crooked Shell

Narrative
Write your own *How the . . . Got His . . .* story; change how the tortoise got his crooked shell; write the dialogue between the birds; write the story as a play script

Poetry
Reptile or animal themed poems: physical features, how they move; poems about flying; shape poems related to animals' shells

UNIT PLAN

Theme: *How the Tortoise Got His Crooked Shell* – Information page   Key Stage 1

FINAL OUTCOME
To write a page for a class information book

PHASE 1

- Read a range of information texts
- Explore and respond – which do you prefer and why? Purpose and audience of each?
- Immerse children in reptile information texts
- Identify information page features (including visual elements such as pictures/diagrams)
- Collect technical vocabulary
- Collect list of writer's hints

Phase 1 outcome

To know what a good information page looks and sounds like

PHASE 2

- Provide stimulus for new reptile information page (hook)
- Explore key vocabulary
- Play word and language games to develop ideas
- Plan information page (including 'design' decisions)
- Orally rehearse ideas
- Refine and/or develop them
- Check plan is complete

Phase 2 outcome

To have planned my information page

PHASE 3

- Model how to use plan to write introduction, and shared write
- Independent write of introductions
- Model how to use plan to write next part of information page, and shared write
- Independent write of next parts
- Redraft elements that need polishing
- Add visuals (e.g. photographs)
- Publish, share and evaluate

UNIT PLAN

Theme: *How the Tortoise Got His Crooked Shell* – **Narrative**

Key Stage 1

FINAL OUTCOME

To write my own *How the Tortoise Got His Crooked Shell* story

PHASE 1

- Read *How the Tortoise Got His Crooked Shell* and respond (likes, dislikes, puzzles, patterns)
- Shared read simple folk tales
- Explore and respond – likes, dislikes, puzzles, patterns
- Collect typical vocabulary and check understanding
- Collect writer's hints for these stories
- Use story map or mountain to chart the key events of *How the Tortoise Got His Crooked Shell*
- Use drama/role play to understand key parts of the plot

Phase 1 outcome

To know the plot and narrative language in *How the Tortoise Got His Crooked Shell* story

PHASE 2

- Discuss other ways that the tortoise's shell could have ended up looking like that
- Use drama/role play to explore ideas
- Collect vocabulary along the way
- Replace main events on story map or mountain with new ideas
- Children create a new story map or plan
- Use word/language games to explore new vocabulary
- Orally rehearse new ideas, including the use of writer's hints
- Finalise plan

Phase 2 outcome

To have planned my story

PHASE 3

- Show children mock-up of final book
- Model write opening – using story map/plan
- Children write opening independently
- Model write main events – using story map/plan
- Children write main events independently
- Model write ending – using story map/plan
- Children write ending independently
- Mark, feed back and edit
- Publish and share

UNIT PLAN

Theme: *How the Tortoise Got His Crooked Shell* – Poetry   Key Stage 1

FINAL OUTCOME
To write and perform reptile-themed poems

PHASE 1

- Read a range of 'creature'-themed poems
- Explore and respond – which do you prefer and why?
- Learn a poem by heart
- Begin to collect list of writer's hints
- Identify features
- Introduce reptile hook
- Direct teach similes and play to develop knowledge and understanding

Phase 1 outcome

To know what good themed poems are and to be able to retell/perform one

PHASE 2

- Use picture/video stimulus to generate ideas
- Play language development games to stimulate and develop vocabulary
- Support children to plan
- Play with similes to ensure that they're used to enhance the poetry

Phase 2 outcome

To have planned my own reptile poem

PHASE 3

- Model how to use plan to write beginning of poem
- Recap expectations around adventurous vocabulary and use of similes
- Independent write of poems
- Publish poems
- Practise performing poems
- Share and perform poems
- Evaluate them

Recount
News reports: grandma rescued from wolf, *Big Bad Wolf Strikes Again*; diaries: Wolf's/LRRH's account of events; letters: Wolf to Grandma, Wolf to LRRH, Grandma to Woodcutter

Description
Settings: woods, LRRH's house, Grandma's house; characters: LRRH, Wolf, Grandma, Woodcutter

Little Red Riding Hood

Narrative
Change the characters; write the story from a different point of view (e.g. Grandma, Wolf); write an up-to-date version; set the story in a city and change the characters

Explanation
How the Big Bad Wolf got his name; safety guide for LRRH or Grandma; Wolf's explanation of why he was at Grandma's; a guide to storybook wolves

UNIT PLAN

Theme: *Little Red Riding Hood* – **Character description**   Key Stage 1

FINAL OUTCOME
To write character descriptions

PHASE 1

- Shared read a variety of character descriptions (preferably known characters such as the Gruffalo, Big Bad Wolf, etc.)
- Compare and contrast – which are effective and why?
- Read *Little Red Riding Hood*
- Write a model character description (of the Big Bad Wolf – physical features and characteristics) and shared read
- Collect writer's hints
- Collect descriptive language and vocabulary
- Introduce task: to write two contrasting character descriptions of grandma (one positive, one negative)

Phase 1 outcome

To know what a good character description sounds like

PHASE 2

- Use picture stimulus to generate ideas and vocabulary about the two different grandmas
- Play word/language games to develop the language of description
- Use role play to support the children with ideas for the character descriptions – physical description and characteristics, and create two short plans
- Pair work – children 'talk' their descriptions
- Play word/language games to continue to develop and rehearse the language of description
- Finalise plans

Phase 2 outcome

To have planned my character descriptions

PHASE 3

- For the first Grandma: model write first couple of lines (including modelling how to work from a plan)
- Children independently write their descriptions
- Share and refine
- Children independently write the second description of Grandma (putting into practice what they have learned from the first)
- Edit, refine and publish

UNIT PLAN

Theme: *Little Red Riding Hood* – Explanation   Key Stage 1

FINAL OUTCOME

To write an explanation on how the Big Bad Wolf got his name

PHASE 1

- Play talk games to establish what an explanation is e.g. explain how you got to school this morning, or why sky is blue
- Shared read simple explanations and identify audience/purpose
- Write model text 'How Little Red Riding Hood got her name' and shared read
- Immerse children in explanation texts, begin to collect writer's hints and unpick language features
- Chunk model text so that children understand structure (what is being explained, main reason why/how, other reasons, conclusion)
- Identify layout features (e.g. diagrams, bullets, headings and purpose of each)

Phase 1 outcome

To know what a good explanation looks and sounds like

PHASE 2

- Read traditional tales featuring 'Big Bad Wolves' and look at illustrations then explain task
- Children generate questions to find out more about the wolf
- Hook: dress up as the Big Bad Wolf and allow children to hot-seat him: Was he always naughty? Does he have any friends? Is he ever good?
- Use phase 1 to map ideas and begin to plan explanations
- Use drama/role play to explore the reasons why Big Bad Wolf is called that (main reason and other reasons)
- Play word/language games to orally rehearse the language of explanation
- Support children to complete their plan

Phase 2 outcome

To have planned my explanation

PHASE 3

- Show children a mock-up of final explanation
- Shared write opening of explanation – model how to use plan
- Children independently write the opening
- Mark and follow up on issues before they move onto the main body of the explanation
- Shared write to support with main body and closing
- Children independently write rest of explanation
- Add additional elements (e.g. headings, diagrams)
- Support them to edit and refine whole text
- Publish, share and evaluate

UNIT PLAN

Theme: *Little Red Riding Hood* – Recount   Key Stage 1

FINAL OUTCOME
To write the Wolf's account as a diary entry

PHASE 1

- Play talk games to establish what a recount is
- Shared read simple recounts
- Compare and contrast; explore and respond – likes, dislikes, puzzles, patterns; and identify audience and purpose of each
- Write a model recount e.g. Little Red Riding Hood's diary entry
- Chunk the model into key events – build a bank of vocabulary for each, and develop children's understanding of this vocabulary
- Use the model to support knowledge of structure and explore the use of time connectives
- Collect writer's hints for a recount
- Hook – find the wolf's diary and wonder what it says about that day

Phase 1 outcome
To know what a good recount sounds like

PHASE 2

- Map each event from the point of view of the wolf
- Use freeze-framing to add detail to each event: How did he feel? etc.
- Collect vocabulary
- Support children to plan their recount
- Play word/language games to orally rehearse the use of time words – children add these to their plan
- Play word/language games to orally rehearse the use of vocabulary to add detail
- Finalise plan

Phase 2 outcome
To have planned my recount

PHASE 3

- Shared write opening of recount – model how to use plan
- Children independently write the opening
- Mark and follow up on issues before they move onto the main body of the recount
- Shared write to support with main body and closing
- Children independently write rest of recount
- Support them to edit and refine whole text
- Publish, share and evaluate

Persuasion
Letters from/to the elves;
adverts; invitations; job adverts
(elf work); catalogue advertising
tiny elf clothes

Description
Describe: the shoemaker,
his shop; the elves, their tiny
clothes, their homes

The Elves and the Shoemaker

Narrative
Write thought bubbles for the
shoemaker and the elves at key
moments; change the setting and
items made; change the ending;
write a new adventure for the
elves; write the story from
the elves' point
of view

Instructions
Safety notices for the elves;
how to make a pair of shoes;
how to spy on an elf; elf
handbook (elf rules/how
to be an elf)

UNIT PLAN

Theme: *The Elves and the Shoemaker* – Instructions   Key Stage 1

FINAL OUTCOME
To write a set of
instructions

PHASE 1

- Hook – read *The Elves and the Shoemaker*
- Explain task – to write an elves handbook
- Shared read various sets of instructions (if possible, look at handbooks; explore and respond; compare and contrast
- Identify the features and typical language of instructions
- Write a model set of instructions (elf themed!), shared read
- Build list of writer's hints for instructions
- Play language games to develop understanding of bossy verb meanings (e.g. mime the action)
- Chunk text into sections and discuss layout (purpose)

Phase 1 outcome
To know what a good
set of instructions looks
and sounds like

PHASE 2

- Play games that involve the children giving instructions to each other; draw out the language and build banks and understanding
- Use pictures/video clips to stimulate ideas
- Use chunks from phase 1 to begin to plan new set of instructions
- Practise use of bossy verbs appropriate to this set of instructions
- Talk activities to support with ideas for what you might put into an introduction, and the 'what you need' section
- Talk activities to support with adding detail into each step
- Support with ideas for a concluding statement
- Complete plan

Phase 2 outcome
To have planned my
instructions

PHASE 3

- Shared write introduction
- Children write introduction and 'what you need' independently
- Shared write initial steps
- Children write steps independently
- Shared write concluding statement
- Children complete independently
- Mark, feed back and edit
- Publish and share (could collate into a class handbook for elves)

UNIT PLAN

Theme: *The Elves and the Shoemaker* – **Narrative**   Key Stage 1

FINAL OUTCOME
To write the story from the point of view of the elves

PHASE 1

- Read *The Elves and the Shoemaker* and respond (likes, dislikes, puzzles, patterns)
- Shared read stories with similar plot patterns
- Explore and respond – likes, dislikes, puzzles, patterns
- Collect writer's hints for these stories
- Use a map or storyboard to chart the plot of *The Elves and the Shoemaker*
- Use drama/role play to understand the key parts of the plot, and to understand how the elves might feel
- Collect vocabulary

Phase 1 outcome
To know the plot and narrative language in *The Elves and the Shoemaker*

PHASE 2

- Use the map to explore what the elves story might be: Where did they come from? How did they know that the shoemaker needed help? Why did they help? How did they feel when they saw their new clothes?
- Support children to start planning, using the mapped structure
- Collect vocabulary along the way
- Role-play and orally rehearse new ideas (the elves' story)
- Practise using elements from the writer's hint list
- Finalise plan

Phase 2 outcome
To have planned my own story

PHASE 3

- Show children mock-up of final book
- Model write opening – using plan
- Children write opening independently
- Model write main events – using plan
- Children write main events independently
- Model write ending – using plan
- Children write ending independently
- Mark, feed back and edit
- Publish and share

UNIT PLAN

Theme: *The Elves and the Shoemaker* – Persuasion

Key Stage 1

FINAL OUTCOME
Persuasive letter

PHASE 1

- Hook – read *The Elves and the Shoemaker*
- Introduce task: to write a letter to the elves persuading them to come to help your mum/dad/carer
- Play talk games to support with understanding what persuasion is
- Shared read and respond to simple letters of persuasion
- Discuss purpose and audience; compare and contrast
- Collect effective vocabulary and language structures
- Chunk a letter into sections so that children understand how it is structured
- Teach letter layout and conventions
- Collect together list of writer's hints for persuasive letters

Phase 1 outcome
To know what persuasion is and what a good persuasive letter looks and sounds like

PHASE 2

- Use drama to help children to explore what they might say to persuade the elves to come and help
- Introduce the vocabulary collected at phase 1 – orally rehearse using this as part of the persuasion
- Support the children to plan their letter by using the chunks from phase 1
- Orally rehearse the letters using elements from the writer's hints
- Finalise plan

Phase 2 outcome
To have planned my persuasive letter

PHASE 3

- Shared write opening of letter – model how to use plan
- Children independently write the opening
- Mark and follow up on issues before they move onto the main body of the letter
- Shared write to support with main body and closing
- Children independently write rest of letter
- Support them to edit and refine whole text
- Publish, share and evaluate
- Send letters to the elves!

Information
Non-fiction book or Wikipedia pages on: lions, jungle animals, jungles, mice, fables, people who help us; thank you letter from the lion

Description
Jungle setting; characters; feelings: fear, trapped, helping others

The Lion and the Mouse

Narrative
Write own version; change the characters; change the setting; write a new fable with the same moral; write the story as a play script; write a sequel where the lion helps the mouse

Persuasion
Wanted poster (lion wants to meet mouse to thank him or her); jungle safety rules poster; adverts for helping others; in role as the mouse, persuade the lion to save the mouse

UNIT PLAN

Theme: *The Lion and the Mouse* – Information   Key Stage 1

FINAL OUTCOME
To write a Wikipedia page on 'people who help us'

PHASE 1

- Read a range of information texts, including Wikipedia pages
- Explore and respond: Which do you prefer and why? Purpose and audience of each?
- Identify Wikipedia page features (including visual elements such as pictures/diagrams) and chunk into sections
- Collect list of writer's hints
- Read *The Lion and the Mouse* and explain task

Phase 1 outcome
To know what a good Wikipedia page looks like

PHASE 2

- Provide stimulus for 'people who like us' theme (hook)
- Explore key vocabulary and check children's understanding
- Using chunks from phase 1 support children to plan Wikipedia page
- Play word and language games to develop ideas
- Orally rehearse ideas
- Refine and/or develop them, considering writer's hints list
- Make page layout and design decisions
- Complete plans

Phase 2 outcome
To have planned my Wikipedia page

PHASE 3

- Model how to use plan to write introduction, and shared write
- Independent write of introductions
- Model how to use plan to write next part of information page, and shared write
- Independent write of next parts
- Redraft elements that need polishing
- Add visuals (e.g. photographs)
- Publish and share

UNIT PLAN

Theme: *The Lion and the Mouse* – Narrative   Key Stage 1

FINAL OUTCOME

To write my own *The Lion and the Mouse* story

PHASE 1

- Read *The Lion and the Mouse* and respond (likes, dislikes, puzzles, patterns)
- Shared read simple fables
- Explore and respond – likes, dislikes, puzzles, patterns
- Collect typical vocabulary and check understanding
- Collect writer's hints for fables
- Use story map or mountain to chart the key events of *The Lion and the Mouse*
- Use drama/role play to understand key parts of the plot, especially the moral

Phase 1 outcome

To know the plot and narrative language in *The Lion and the Mouse*

PHASE 2

- Discuss other ways that the mouse could have helped the lion
- Use drama/role play to explore ideas
- Collect vocabulary along the way
- Replace main events on story map or mountain with new ideas
- Children create a new story map or plan
- Use word/language games to explore new vocabulary
- Orally rehearse new ideas, including the use of writer's hints
- Finalise plan

Phase 2 outcome

To have planned my story

PHASE 3

- Show children mock-up of final book
- Model write opening – using story map/plan
- Children write opening independently
- Model write main events – using story map/plan
- Children write main events independently
- Model write ending – using story map/plan
- Children write ending independently
- Mark, feed back and edit
- Publish and share

UNIT PLAN

Theme: *The Lion and the Mouse* – Persuasion

Key Stage 1

FINAL OUTCOME
'Wanted' persuasive poster

PHASE 1

- Hook – watch TV adverts around a theme (e.g. toys, cars)
- General discussion re: adverts – purpose and audience?
- Look at and discuss information/persuasive posters
- Discuss purpose and audience; compare and contrast
- Write a model 'wanted' poster and support the children to learn the text to internalise language
- Collect effective vocabulary and language structures
- Discuss any relevant design features (which children may use on their own posters)

Phase 1 outcome

To know what persuasion is and what a good persuasive poster looks and sounds like

PHASE 2

- Read *The Lion and the Mouse* and explain that the lion wants to find the mouse to thank him/her
- Ask the children to come up with ideas of how he could use adverts to find the mouse
- Use drama to help children to explore what they might say to people to persuade them to help find the mouse
- Introduce the vocabulary collected at phase 1 – orally rehearse using this as part of the persuasion
- Support children to decide on what their posters will say
- Orally rehearse and finalise ideas

Phase 2 outcome

To have planned my persuasive poster

PHASE 3

- Shared write the poster
- Independent and guided write posters
- Share, evaluate and redraft to ensure message is clear
- Make final design decisions (e.g. size of text, page layout, inclusion of photographs, etc.)
- Publish and evaluate for overall impact of poster

Recount
Science reports on changing states (heating/cooling); newspaper reports; letters about the events; gossip magazine interview about the events

Description
Describe the character that gave the pot; describe food in various states; use senses to describe food

The Magic Porridge Pot

Narrative
Change the: setting, characters, container, food that is in the pot; change the opening – why the main character is given the pot; change how to get the pot to stop; change the ending to an unhappy one

Instructions
Porridge recipes; oats recipes; instructions for an everlasting pot of . . . (different food to porridge); instruction manual for the magic porridge pot

UNIT PLAN

Theme: *The Magic Porridge Pot* – Instructions

Key Stage 1

FINAL OUTCOME

To write a set of instructions (porridge recipe)

PHASE 1

- Hook – read *The Magic Porridge Pot*
- Ask the children if they've ever eaten porridge; discuss how it is made
- Task: to write a set of instructions for making porridge (recipe)
- Shared read various sets of instructions and recipes
- Explore and respond – compare and contrast
- Identify the features and typical language of recipes (e.g. introduction, what you need, what you do, bossy verbs, ordered steps, concluding statement)
- Build list of writer's hints for recipes
- Play language games to develop understanding of bossy verb meanings (e.g. mime the action), focusing on cookery-related verbs
- Discuss the layout of a recipe – look at real recipe books as well as on-screen
- Decide on the best layout for your recipe writing

Phase 1 outcome

To know what a good set of instructions looks and sounds like

PHASE 2

- Support children to make porridge; take photographs as they do
- Use photographs to support with planning recipe writing
- Practise use of bossy verbs appropriate to this set of instructions
- Talk activities to support with ideas for what you might put into an introduction and conclusion
- Talk activities to support with ideas for adding detail into each step (e.g. take the pan off the heat and carefully stir in the oats)
- Complete plan

Phase 2 outcome

To have planned my instructions

PHASE 3

- Shared write introduction
- Children write introduction and 'what you need' independently
- Shared write initial steps
- Children write steps independently
- Shared write concluding statement
- Children complete independently
- Mark, feed back and edit
- Publish and share

UNIT PLAN

Theme: *The Magic Porridge Pot* – Narrative   Key Stage 1

FINAL OUTCOME
To write *The Magic . . . Pot* story

PHASE 1

- Read The Magic Porridge Pot story and respond (likes, dislikes, puzzles, patterns)
- Chunk it into sections so that children can see the pattern and plot
- Reread *The Magic Porridge Pot* regularly so that the children internalise language and sentence structures
- Collect effective vocabulary and language – check understanding of effect
- Build list of writer's hints

Phase 1 outcome
To know *The Magic Porridge Pot* story and what makes it a good story

PHASE 2

- Discuss another food that could be in a magic pot
- Use picture stimulus to support ideas
- Use drama/role play to explore new events
- Collect vocabulary along the way
- Map or plan new story
- Use word/language games to orally rehearse new vocabulary and language
- Orally rehearse new story
- Finalise plan

Phase 2 outcome
To have planned my story

PHASE 3

- Show children mock-up of final book
- Model write opening – using plan
- Children write opening independently
- Model write main events – using plan
- Children write main events independently
- Model write ending – using story plan
- Children write ending independently
- Mark, feed back and edit
- Publish and share

UNIT PLAN

Theme: *The Magic Porridge Pot* – **Recount**   Key Stage 1

FINAL OUTCOME

Magazine article recounting the events of *The Magic Porridge Pot*

PHASE 1

- Play talk games to establish what a recount is
- Shared read simple recounts
- Compare and contrast; explore and respond – likes, dislikes, puzzles, patterns; identify audience and purpose of each
- Write a model text that recounts the events from a story (e.g. *Cinderella*), include quotes from characters (as if they have been interviewed)
- Chunk the model into key events – build a bank of vocabulary for each, and develop children's understanding of this vocabulary
- Use the model to support knowledge of structure and explore the use of time connectives
- Collect writer's hints for a recount
- Read *The Magic Porridge Pot*

Phase 1 outcome

To know what a good recount sounds like

PHASE 2

- Explain task
- Hook – dress up as one of the characters from the story; children hot-seat you to establish what happened and how you felt
- Support the children to sequence and map the main events
- Use freeze-framing to add detail to each event – you may need to hot-seat other characters
- Collect vocabulary
- Support children to plan their recount
- Play word/language games to orally rehearse the use of time words – children add these to their plan
- Finalise plan

Phase 2 outcome

To have planned my recount

PHASE 3

- Shared write opening of recount – model how to use plan
- Children independently write the opening
- Mark and follow up on issues before they move onto the main body of the recount
- Shared write to support with main body and closing
- Children independently write rest of recount
- Support them to edit and refine whole text
- Publish, share and evaluate

Recount
Diary entries from different viewpoints (e.g. Miss Cackle, Miss Hardbroom, Ethel, Maud); news report on the Halloween celebrations; spells write-up

Description
Characters: Miss Cackle, Miss Hardbroom, Mildred, Maud; setting: the academy, Mildred's room

The Worst Witch
by Jill Murphy

Narrative
Prequel: Agatha's revenge; change the ending: Mildred gets expelled! Add an event to the story; add thought bubbles to key moments; write a key moment as a short play script

Instructions
Spells in *The Popular Book of Spells*; how to fly a broomstick; how to please Miss Hardbroom; invisibility potion; following the Witches' Code

UNIT PLAN

Theme: *The Worst Witch* – Setting descriptions

Key Stage 1

FINAL OUTCOME
To write two setting descriptions

PHASE 1

- Shared read known stories and use them to discuss what 'settings' are
- Shared read and immerse children in a variety of good-quality setting descriptions
- Collect list of writer's hints for setting descriptions
- Play word/language games to develop the language of description
- Chunk a setting description into parts so that children understand structure
- Hook – read extracts from *The Worst Witch* that describe the academy
- Collect vocabulary from the book to build a picture of the academy

Phase 1 outcome
To know what a good setting description sounds like

PHASE 2

- Support the children to create a story map, or plan, for describing the academy
- Pair work – children 'talk' their descriptions (use collected vocabulary effectively)
- Play word/language games to continue to develop and rehearse the language of description
- Complete plan (or story map)
- Using the process in phase 3 write/edit descriptions
- Carry out the same process as above but for your own school setting
- Rehearse using language collected in phase 1 and use games to develop ideas
- Complete second plan

Phase 2 outcome
To have planned my two setting descriptions

PHASE 3

- For the academy: model write first couple of lines (including modelling how to work from a plan)
- Children independently write their descriptions
- Share and refine
- Children independently write their descriptions of their school setting (putting into practice what they have learned from the academy descriptions)
- Edit, refine and publish

UNIT PLAN

Theme: *The Worst Witch* – Newspaper reports

Key Stage 1

FINAL OUTCOME
Newspaper report on the Halloween celebrations

PHASE 1

- Hook – watch children's TV news report
- General discussion re news reports – purpose and audience
- Talk activities to explore what our 'news' is
- Shared read age-appropriate newspaper reports and respond
- Immerse children in newspaper reports so that they internalise the language patterns
- Discuss how stories are handled/portrayed
- Check understanding of purpose and audience of newspaper reports
- Collect list of writer's hints, and appropriate vocabulary
- Chunk newspaper report into sections to check understanding of typical structure (headline, '5 W's intro para, story para, background/eyewitness para, concluding para)

Phase 1 outcome

To know what a good newspaper report looks and sounds like

PHASE 2

- Reread Chapter 6 (the Halloween celebrations)
- Explore key events through drama/freeze-framing and hot-seating
- Create a plan
- Explore headline to use
- Orally rehearse the key events to be reported on, using language collected in phase 1; add ideas to plan
- Finalise plan

Phase 2 outcome

To have planned my newspaper report

PHASE 3

- Shared write opening, including headline and use of language
- Children independently write openings
- Shared write next parts picking up on issues as report progresses
- Children independently write next parts
- Peer evaluate success, then edit
- Publish

UNIT PLAN

Theme: *The Worst Witch* – Play script

Key Stage 1

FINAL OUTCOME

To write a play script of a scene from *The Worst Witch*

PHASE 1

- Shared read short plays (start with known stories, e.g. *traditional tales*)
- Discuss and check understanding of what a play script is – purpose and audience
- Children act out short scenes – turn them into short-burst play scripts by shared writing
- Shared read play scripts and analyse for features
- Collect writer's hints for play scripts and key vocabulary

Phase 1 outcome

To know what a play script is and the features of a good one

PHASE 2

- Hook – reread the part of Chapter 3 when Mildred turns Ethel into a pig
- Check children's understanding of this part of the story
- Use drama to act it out: What is said? What do the characters do? Any extra detail?
- Freeze-frame and discuss how to record as a play script
- Collect vocabulary for narrations/stage directions
- Orally rehearse – practise using writer's hints
- Plan play script

Phase 2 outcome

To have planned my play script

PHASE 3

- Shared write play script
- Children independently write play script
- Support with editing and refining
- Perform, share and evaluate

Mind maps
and unit plans

Recount
Diary entries; significant moments as recounts (e.g. driving the Mini); letters; Danny's autobiography/Danny's biography written by his father William

Description
Character descriptions of Danny/William/Victor Hazell; setting descriptions of Danny's home and the woods

Danny, the Champion of the World
by Roald Dahl

Narrative
Play script: significant moment of the story; court trial for poaching; write a new adventure that could be inserted into the story; a short story prequel or sequel

Explanation
How to catch a pheasant (use one of Danny's father's methods or make up a new one); how to be a poacher; how to live in a caravan; about poachers; the plan to catch 200 pheasants

UNIT PLAN

Theme: *Danny, the Champion of the World* – Explanation   Key Stage 2

FINAL OUTCOME
To write an explanation of how to catch a pheasant

PHASE 1

- Shared read explanation texts
- Compare and contrast; explore and respond; begin to build list of writer's hints
- Unpick language features and understand why they are used/effective
- Build word bank of technical vocabulary (short write glossary) and other 'explanation'-type words/phrases
- Check understanding of the structure of the explanation text – heading, introduction, paragraph content, conclusion, diagrams/pictures
- Discuss layout (purpose)
- Finalise list of writer's hints

Phase 1 outcome
To know what a good explanation text looks and sounds like

PHASE 2

- Hook – reread extracts of *Danny* where methods of catching pheasants are described and introduce task (invent purpose and audience)
- Use hook and picture/video stimulus to discuss technical vocabulary needed for writing explanation
- Begin to build list of technical vocabulary
- Orally rehearse explanations
- Play word and language games to practise using 'explanation'-type words/phrases in context
- Create plan then make decisions about layout – what goes where on the page and why?

Phase 2 outcome
To have planned my own explanation text

PHASE 3

- Model write introduction
- Children write own
- Shared write first paragraph
- Children write own
- Support with decisions about next paragraph, including layout
- Children complete the rest of their explanations
- Mark, feed back and edit
- Publish and share
- Evaluate

UNIT PLAN

Theme: *Danny, the Champion of the World* – Play script   Key Stage 2

FINAL OUTCOME

To write a play script based on *Danny, the Champion of the World*

PHASE 1

- Hook – after reading *Danny*, explain that he and his father are arrested for poaching; discuss
- Introduce task: to write a play script of the court case that ensued
- Read short plays and analyse for the conventions
- Compare and contrast (look for which are more effectively written and why)
- Collect vocabulary from narrations/stage directions
- Build list of writer's hints for play scripts
- Read the courtroom scene from *Toad of Toad Hall* (A.A. Milne) – respond

Phase 1 outcome

To know the features and conventions of play scripts

PHASE 2

- Using the *Toad of Toad Hall* scene as a stimulus, use drama to support children to think through the events of *Danny's* court scene: How will it start? End? What will happen in the middle? Any big moments?
- Freeze-frame key moments, collect vocabulary, refine ideas – check that dialogue effectively portrays characters
- Storyboard (as plan) and add vocabulary
- Collect vocabulary for narrations/stage directions
- Orally rehearse and add to storyboard
- Finalise

Phase 2 outcome

To have planned my play script

PHASE 3

- Shared write play script opening
- Children independently write opening
- Mark, feed back and support with editing as required
- Using shared writing to model when necessary, support children to complete play scripts
- Perform and evaluate

UNIT PLAN

Theme: *Danny, the Champion of the World* – Recount (diary)   Key Stage 2

FINAL OUTCOME
To write Danny's diary entries of events

PHASE 1

- Shared read diary entries/extracts (avoid ones that are too informal – remember that these are models for writing)
- Compare and contrast; explore and respond – likes, dislikes, puzzles, patterns; and identify purpose of each
- Build a list of writer's hints for diaries (avoid an overemphasis on 'informal language')
- Chunk a diary entry into parts to support with structure
- Hook – read extracts of key events for Danny

Phase 1 outcome
To know what a good diary entry sounds like

PHASE 2

- Support the children to think through how one of the events would be recorded in Danny's diary
- Hot-seat Danny to establish how he felt, and other details
- Collect vocabulary (including time connectives to structure the recount)
- Children complete their plan
- Play word/language games to orally rehearse the use of time words and the use of vocabulary to add detail – children add these to their plan
- Follow the same process again for a different event so that children have two complete plans

Phase 2 outcome
To have planned my diary entries

PHASE 3

- Carry out the following process for both diary entries:
- Shared write opening of diary entry – model how to use plan
- Children independently write the opening
- Mark and follow up on issues before they move onto the main body of the diary entry
- Shared write to support with main body and closing
- Children independently write rest of diary entry
- Support them to edit and refine whole text
- Publish, share and evaluate

NB: Check what learning has taken place that will inform the writing of the second diary entry before starting it

Information
Contrasting reports on the culture of Lila's country compared to yours; a report on the Firework Festival; an information leaflet about the Firework Festival; international firework festivals

Description
Characters: Lalchand; Lila; Chulak; Razvani the Fire-Fiend; Hamlet the elephant; Rambashi; settings: Mt Merapi; firework descriptions

The Firework Maker's Daughter
by Philip Pullman

Narrative
Write a new Lila's quest story; write a wishing tale; write the story from Lalchand's viewpoint; write the sequel; write a new adventure for Rambashi

Instructions
Firework making; firework safety rules; how to succeed at a quest; Razvani's Fire-Fiend instructions; recipe for a firework festival; firework festival poster/ sign

UNIT PLAN

Theme: *The Firework Maker's Daughter* – **Information**   Key Stage 2

FINAL OUTCOME
Firework Festival
information leaflet

PHASE 1

- Shared read a variety of information texts (ideally about festivals/carnivals)
- Compare and contrast; explore and respond – likes, dislikes, puzzles, patterns; and identify purpose and audience of each
- Begin to collect writer's hints (including persuasive techniques)
- Immerse the children in information leaflets so that they internalise the language patterns
- Collect effective language and vocabulary
- Chunk an information leaflet into sections to analyse structure, check understanding of purpose of each section

Phase 1 outcome
To know what a good information leaflet looks and sounds like

PHASE 2

- Hook – watch film clips of firework festivals and explain task
- Use film and photographs to collect effective language and vocabulary and add to list from phase 1
- Use chunks from phase 1 to start to plan leaflet
- Research firework festivals to collect facts and interesting information
- Use talk activities to support with the development, and oral rehearsal, of ideas for each section of the plan
- Finalise plan
- Consider design aspects: How will they lay out their leaflet? Will they add any photographs? Extra text?

Phase 2 outcome
To have planned my information leaflet

PHASE 3

- Shared write opening section of leaflet
- Children independently write opening section
- Mark, and support children to edit, refine and evaluate
- Shared write other sections of leaflet, where necessary
- Children independently write other sections
- Edit and refine to check for impact on reader
- Add design elements – check that the leaflet is as visually effective as possible
- Publish, share and evaluate

UNIT PLAN

Theme: *The Firework Maker's Daughter* – Instructions   Key Stage 2

FINAL OUTCOME

To write a safety poster for a fireworks festival

PHASE 1

- Hook – watch film clips of firework festivals and explain task
- Shared read various safety/information posters
- Explore and respond – compare and contrast
- Identify the features and typical language used
- Begin to collect vocabulary
- Learn model poster (must be similar to 'festival safety') by heart
- Collect writer's hints for a safety poster

Phase 1 outcome

To know what a safety poster looks and sounds like

PHASE 2

- Use talk activities to explore the aspects that might be covered on the safety poster
- Collect further vocabulary and add to list
- Generate effective imperative verbs and play with them to help decide on the most appropriate for the poster
- Begin to complete plan
- Support with ideas for a concluding statement
- Support children to make design decisions so that the poster is eye-catching
- Complete plan

Phase 2 outcome

To have planned my poster

PHASE 3

- Shared write first part of poster
- Children write rest of poster independently
- Mark, feed back and edit
- Add design features
- Publish and share

UNIT PLAN

Theme: *The Firework Maker's Daughter* – **Narrative**   Key Stage 2

FINAL OUTCOME
To write a new Lila's quest story

PHASE 1

- Hook – make up a hook into a new quest for Lila (e.g. letter, video message, email)
- Shared read a range of quest stories, respond – likes, dislikes, puzzles, patterns
- Collect language and vocabulary that are effective
- Use a map or story mountain to outline the basic plot of a quest story
- Collect list of writer's hints
- Chunk Lila's quest from *The Firework Maker's Daughter* so that children understand the plot structure

Phase 1 outcome
To know what a good quest story looks and sounds like

PHASE 2

- Support children to think about the new quest for Lila: What might happen along the way? Who will she meet? Good? Evil? How will it end?
- Use talk activities and drama/role play to add detail to (1) main events and (2) any new characters
- Begin to plan ideas
- Support children to plan how they will incorporate elements of the writer's hints
- Orally rehearse main events using vocabulary and language collected at phase 1
- Finalise plan

Phase 2 outcome
To have planned my quest story

PHASE 3

- Shared write opening to get the writing process started
- Children independently write the opening and build up paragraphs
- Mark and follow-up on issues before they move onto the problem and resolution parts
- Shared write/children independently write problem, resolution and ending
- Support them to edit and refine story
- Publish, share and evaluate

Recount
Letters: to/from Michael's parents; reply to Kensuke's son; log entries; Kensuke's biography; message in a bottle; events from different viewpoints

Description
The Peggy Sue; Kensuke's cave house; the island; the changing seas; the characters

Kensuke's Kingdom
by Michael Morpurgo

Narrative
I disappeared on the night before my twelfth birthday story; desert island story; change the ending; write a sequel (Michael or Kensuke); add a chapter; rewrite a scene from a different viewpoint; write a scene as a play script

Explanation
How to survive on a desert island; how to make a shelter on a desert island; how to hunt/poach; what to take to a desert island; how to make a sea vessel from raw materials on a desert island

UNIT PLAN

Theme: *Kensuke's Kingdom* – Explanation   Upper Key Stage 2

FINAL OUTCOME

To write an explanation of how to survive on a desert island

PHASE 1

- Shared read explanation texts
- Compare and contrast; explore and respond; begin to build list of writer's hints
- Learn by heart a paragraph of an explanation text (e.g. 'How to survive on a . . .')
- Unpick language features and understand why they are used/effective
- Build word bank of technical vocabulary (short write glossary) and other 'explanation'-type words/phrases
- Check understanding of the structure of the explanation text
- Finalise list of writer's hints

Phase 1 outcome

To know what a good explanation text looks and sounds like

PHASE 2

- Hook – watch film clips of desert island survival tips e.g. Ray Mears, Bear Grylls, introduce explanation task
- Use hook and picture stimulus, and relevant text extracts to discuss technical vocabulary needed for writing explanation
- Begin to build list of technical vocabulary
- Use talk activities to support children to expand ideas on how to survive on a desert island – what will their paragraph content be?
- Play word and language games to practise using 'explanation'-type words/phrases in context; orally rehearse explanations
- Create new plan, including technical vocabulary to be used
- Make decisions about layout – what goes where on page?

Phase 2 outcome

To have planned my own explanation text

PHASE 3

- Shared write introduction
- Children write own independently
- Shared write first paragraph
- Children write own independently
- Continue until children complete the main body of their explanations
- Shared write conclusion
- Children write own independently
- Mark, feed back and edit
- Turn polished piece into a designed final explanation text
- Publish and share
- Evaluate

UNIT PLAN

Theme: *Kensuke's Kingdom* – **Narrative**   Upper Key Stage 2

FINAL OUTCOME

To write a flashback story using the first line of *Kensuke's Kingdom*

PHASE 1

- Read a range of short stories with flashbacks
- Explore purpose and audience for each
- Explore likes, dislikes, puzzles, patterns for each
- Use mapping to identify typical plot structure to these types of stories, and where the flashback sits (e.g. flashback/opening, build-up, problem, resolution, ending *or* opening, build-up, flashback)
- Check that children are clear about how flashback is used to best effect – explore this if necessary – using language games
- Collect writer's hints – tools that make a good flashback story
- Collect effective language or vocabulary

Phase 1 outcome

To know what a good flashback story sounds like

PHASE 2

- Hook: read the first line of *Kensuke's Kingdom*; task: to tell your own story, which starts 'I disappeared on the night before my twelfth birthday'
- Use drama and role play to guide thinking through (1) main events and (2) how characters might feel and react (description/action/dialogue to portray this)
- Create individual story maps, boards or plans
- Use drama to add to ideas around action/dialogue; add to story maps, boards or plans
- Orally rehearse use of collected language
- Finalise plans

Phase 2 outcome

To have planned my flashback story

PHASE 3

- Brief shared writing opening to model expectations
- Children independently write the first two sections of the story
- Mark and follow up on issues before they move onto the next parts
- Shared write to support, where necessary – especially the flashback part
- Children independently write rest of story
- Support them to edit and refine story
- Publish, share and evaluate

UNIT PLAN

Theme: *Kensuke's Kingdom* – Recount (ship's log)   Upper Key Stage 2

FINAL OUTCOME
To write Michael's parents' log of the days after he went missing

PHASE 1

- Hook – reread extracts from the 'Ship's Log' chapter and respond (likes/dislikes/puzzles/patterns)
- Introduce task
- Carefully shared read and analyse the ship's log entries drawing out the details that are given, the mood and how it is depicted, etc.
- Build a list of writer's hints for logs such as these
- Chunk a log into parts to support with structure
- Collect vocabulary and language

Phase 1 outcome

To know what a good ship's log looks and sounds like

PHASE 2

- Support the children to imagine what happens to Michael's parents when they realise he has gone: come up with four key events
- Use freeze-framing/hot-seating/role play to work through each event and discuss where they were, what they were doing and how they felt at each point
- Collect vocabulary and language
- Children complete a plan for each event
- Play word/language games to orally rehearse the vocabulary and language of a ship's log
- Finalise plans

Phase 2 outcome

To have planned my ship's log

PHASE 3

- Shared write opening of first log
- Children independently write the first log
- Mark and follow up on issues before they move onto the next log
- Shared write to support where necessary
- Children independently write rest of logs
- Support them to edit and refine logs
- Publish, share and evaluate

Recount
Biography: George; Gordon Barraclough; Bobby Charlton; newspaper report: unexpected invitation to tea; diary entries; recount of events from others' viewpoints; match commentaries

Description
Characters: him in his uncle's football kit; his mum; Gordon Barraclough; Mr Melrose; settings: Christmas lights; town hall

The Fib
by George Layton

Narrative
Write a new version of *The Fib* set in the present day; write it from Barraclough's point of view; change the ending; change the fib; write a completely new *The Fib* story; play script of the scene in the Lord Mayor's parlour

Discussion
Corporal punishment; discipline in schools; Is fibbing ever acceptable? Is Gordon Barraclough a bully?

UNIT PLAN

Theme: *The Fib* – Recount (biography)   Upper Key Stage 2

FINAL OUTCOME
To write a biography based on *The Fib*

PHASE 1

- Shared read biographies from Marcia Williams's *Three Cheers for Inventors*
- Respond – likes, dislikes, puzzles, patterns; and identify purpose and audience
- General discussion re: biographies – check children understand the purpose and audience
- Immerse the children in short biographies
- Identify use of language, collect and create list of writer's hints
- Chunk a simple biography into sections (opening, childhood paragraph(s), later life paragraph(s), conclusion) so that children understand structure

Phase 1 outcome
To know what a good biography sounds like

PHASE 2

- Hook – use *The Fib* as a stimulus
- Hot-seat George, his mum, etc. to find out about his life
- Begin to put together a timeline
- Use talk/drama activities to decide on extra detail, especially around his later life: Did *The Fib* change his life? How? What did he go on to achieve?
- Use chunks from phase 1 to help plan biography
- Orally rehearse use of effective language (collected in phase 1)
- Add to plan, and finalise

Phase 2 outcome
To have planned my biography

PHASE 3

- Shared write opening
- Independent and guided write openings
- Shared write next parts picking up on issues as biography progresses
- Support with concluding paragraph – check it has impact
- Check that the biography has a sensible chronological order and is interesting to read
- Edit and evaluate
- Publish

UNIT PLAN

Theme: *The Fib* – Discussion   Upper Key Stage 2

FINAL OUTCOME
To write a discussion about corporal punishment

PHASE 1

- Read a range of discussion texts (factual rather than persuasive and emotive)
- Explore purpose and audience for each; agree basic principles of these kinds of discussions
- Use talk activities to further explore the concept of 'discussion'
- Collect list of writer's hints
- Play language games to practise using discursive language
- Chunk a discursive text into sections to clarify structure of discussion texts (paragraphs: intro, points for, points against, conclusion)

Phase 1 outcome
To know what good discussion texts look and sound like

PHASE 2

- Hook – a letter about bringing back corporal punishment, or similar (something that gets the children fired up about the topic!)
- Introduce the task: to write a discussion about corporal punishment
- Use chunks from phase 1 to start to plan new discussion
- Use research- and discussion-based activities to explore arguments for and against corporal punishment
- Use language games to further explore the effective use of discursive language, and weave this through the arguments already established
- Complete plan

Phase 2 outcome
To have planned my own discussion text

PHASE 3

- Shared write introduction and points for paragraph(s)
- Children independently write introduction and points for paragraph(s)
- Shared write points against and concluding paragraphs
- Children independently write points against and concluding paragraphs
- Support with editing and refining discussions
- Share and evaluate (including relating back to initial hook)

UNIT PLAN

Theme: *The Fib* – **Narrative**   Upper Key Stage 2

FINAL OUTCOME
To write *The Fib* story from Barraclough's point of view

PHASE 1

- Read *The Fib* and respond (likes, dislikes, puzzles, patterns)
- Use storyboard, mountain or map as a visual prompt to the key events
- Use freeze-framing to support children to understand the key events of the story
- Familiarise the children with the plot so that they can retell it in summary form
- Shared read stories from different viewpoints (e.g. *The True Story of the 3 Little Pigs*; *Seriously, Cinderella Is So Annoying*)
- Explore and respond – likes, dislikes, puzzles, patterns
- Collect list of writer's hints for these stories
- Collect effective vocabulary and typical language from *The Fib*

Phase 1 outcome
To know *The Fib* story and what a good story from an alternative viewpoint sounds like

PHASE 2

- Use drama/freeze-framing to explore the plot from the point of view of Gordon Barraclough – special focus on the fib part
- Create a new storyboard of the main events
- Hot-seat Barraclough to discover how he feels; to add additional information to the new story/plot, especially the fib and the ending
- Add to storyboard, then transfer to a plan
- Use word/language games to explore new vocabulary
- Orally rehearse new ideas, weaving in language collected at phase 1
- Finalise plan

Phase 2 outcome
To have planned my story

PHASE 3

- Model write opening – using story map/plan
- Children write opening independently
- Model write main events – using story map/plan (the fib must be a high focus)
- Children write main events independently
- Model write ending – using story map/plan (high focus)
- Children write ending independently
- Mark, feedback and edit
- Publish, share and evaluate

Information
Fact files: each character; each setting; the magic ring; hobbits; elves; trolls; character top trump cards; travel brochure style information pages; tourist guides; glossary of terms

Description
Characters: Bilbo Baggins; Smaug; Gandalf; Gollum; settings: Bag-End; Rivendell; the Misty Mountains; Mirkwood; the Lonely Mountain

The Hobbit
by J.R.R. Tolkien

Narrative
Write your own hobbit adventure using the book's opening words; magic ring story; write Gollum's story; write one of the main events from a different viewpoint; write a new story with the trolls or Smaug as the main character(s); write a new story set in one of the places in *The Hobbit*

Instructions
How to travel to . . . (e.g. the Lonely Mountain); how to look after a hobbit; Gandalf's Guide to . . .; Hobbit rules; Smaug rules; Gandalf's recipes; how to use the magic ring

UNIT PLAN

Theme: *The Hobbit* – Information   Key Stage 2

FINAL OUTCOME
Tourist guide entries

PHASE 1

- Shared read a variety of tourist guide information texts
- Compare and contrast; explore and respond – likes, dislikes, puzzles, patterns; and identify purpose and audience of each
- Begin to collect writer's hints (including persuasive techniques)
- Immerse the children in information leaflets so that they internalise the language patterns (can create and shared read a model about Bag-End or Rivendell)
- Collect effective language and vocabulary
- Chunk a tourist guide into sections to analyse structure, check understanding of purpose of each section
- Add to writer's hints

Phase 1 outcome

To know what a good tourist guide looks and sounds like

PHASE 2

- Hook – read descriptions, and look at pictures, of key settings from *The Hobbit*
- Collect effective language and vocabulary and add to list from phase 1
- Use talk activities to support with the development, and oral rehearsal, of ideas for each section of the plan
- Finalise plan for first entry
- Consider design aspects: How will they lay out their guide? Will they add any photographs? Extra text?
- Now repeat the planning process (including design) for the second entry to the guide and finalise plan

Phase 2 outcome

To have planned my tourist guide entries

PHASE 3

- Shared write beginning of first tourist guide entry
- Children independently write first entry
- Mark, and support children to edit, refine and evaluate first entry
- Support to change plans for second entry in the light of any new information from first entry
- Shared write beginning of second tourist guide entry
- Children independently write second entry
- Edit and refine to check for impact on reader
- Publish, share and evaluate

UNIT PLAN

Theme: *The Hobbit* – Instructions

Key Stage 2

FINAL OUTCOME
To write a set of instructions

PHASE 1

- Hook – reread parts of *The Hobbit* that mention Bilbo's use of the magic ring
- Explain task – to make up, and then write, a set of instructions for how to use the magic ring
- Shared read various sets of instructions
- Explore and respond – compare and contrast
- Identify the features and typical language of instructions (e.g. introduction, what you need, what you do, imperative verbs, ordered steps, concluding statement)
- Collect writer's hints for instructions

Phase 1 outcome
To know what a good set of instructions looks and sounds like

PHASE 2

- Hot-seat Bilbo and Gandalf to ask for advice on using the magic ring
- Use drama and freeze-framing of key moments in the story to support children to think through what might be good advice for how to use the magic ring
- Orally rehearse and then plan each step for the 'what you do' box; remember to add detail into each step
- Use talk activities/drama to support with ideas for what you might put into the 'what you need' section e.g. a coat with a hidden pocket at the hip; add to plan
- Use talk activities to support with ideas for what you might put into an introduction
- Support with ideas for a concluding statement
- Complete plan

Phase 2 outcome
To have planned my instructions

PHASE 3

- Shared write introduction
- Children write introduction and 'what you need' independently
- Shared write initial steps
- Children write steps independently
- Shared write concluding statement
- Children complete independently
- Mark, feed back and edit
- Publish, share and evaluate

UNIT PLAN

Theme: *The Hobbit* – **Narrative**   Key Stage 2

FINAL OUTCOME

To write a good versus evil story – the story of Smaug's capture of the Lonely Mountain

PHASE 1

- Read a range of short stories with good versus evil as the underlying theme
- Respond to and explore purpose and audience for each
- Collect good versus evil vocabulary
- Use mapping or a story mountain to identify typical plot structure to these types of stories (i.e. opening, build-up, problem, resolution, ending)
- Check that children are clear about 'suspense', which is usually used in the build-up and problem parts – explore this if necessary – using language games; build writer's hints

Phase 1 outcome

To know what a good versus evil story sounds like

PHASE 2

- Hook: reread the part where Baggins first sees Smaug
- Use drama to explore and imagine the 'story' behind Smaug attacking the dwarves and surrounding people of the Lonely Mountain
- Ensure children are secure about (1) the build-up to Smaug attacking, (2) the attack itself and (3) how Smaug wins
- Orally rehearse ideas, weaving in vocabulary and language collected earlier
- Begin to plan, children should have decided whether Smaug is good or evil, and therefore which 'wins through')
- Use talk activities to think through the opening and ending sections
- Finalise plan

Phase 2 outcome

To have planned my good versus evil story

PHASE 3

- Mock-up finished Smaug storybook so that children can picture their end product
- Brief shared write to get children started
- Children independently write the opening and build-up paragraphs
- Mark and follow up on issues before they move onto the problem and resolution parts
- Shared write to support, where necessary
- Children independently write rest of story, including the ending
- Support them to edit and refine story
- Publish, share and evaluate

Recount
Newspaper reports; eyewitness reports on the arrival of the Iron Man/ key events; Hogarth's journal; the Iron Man's journal; scientific experiment (e.g. materials)

Description
Iron Man: compared to others; movement; eating; characteristics; Space Being; Hogarth; settings: cliff/beach; scrapyard; farms

The Iron Man by Ted Hughes

Narrative
Write a prequel or sequel about *The Iron Man*; write the *Space Being* story; change the ending; write another 'beat the monster' story involving the Iron Giant; write the story from the Giant's viewpoint

Information
Diet: Iron Man; Space Being; guide to looking after an Iron Man; non-chronological report: The Iron Man; Space Being

UNIT PLAN

Theme: *The Iron Man* – **Information**   Lower Key Stage 2

FINAL OUTCOME

Non-chronological report about *The Iron Man*

PHASE 1

- Hook – watch short clips from *The Iron Giant* film that give information about *The Iron Man*
- Introduce task – invent purpose and decide on audience
- Use talk activities to get the children thinking about the most interesting parts of *The Iron Man* that could go into a report (bearing in mind audience)
- Chunk a simple non-chronological report to establish the structure of a report
- Immerse children in the text type by reading and analysing other non-chronological reports
- Identify key features and collect effective language and vocabulary
- Discuss most effective layout
- Collect writer's hints

Phase 1 outcome

To know what a good non-chronological report looks and sounds like

PHASE 2

- Using chunked report from phase 1, decide on the key topics in the main body of the report (e.g. what he looks like, what he eats, etc.)
- In addition to text extracts, use drama and talk activities to develop ideas around each topic
- Orally rehearse use of appropriate and effective language
- Create plan
- Support children to make design decisions: What will their report look like on the page? Are they going to add any pictures? Where will they go? Why?
- Orally rehearse opening and concluding paragraph ideas

Phase 2 outcome

To have planned my non-chronological report

PHASE 3

- Shared write opening paragraph – model how to use the plan as a guide
- Independent and guided writing opening paragraphs
- Shared write next parts picking up on issues as report progresses
- Support with polishing final draft, including design decisions (add pictures if required)
- Edit and evaluate
- Publish

UNIT PLAN

Theme: *The Iron Man* – Narrative   Lower Key Stage 2

FINAL OUTCOME
To write an Iron Man 'beat the monster' story

PHASE 1

- Read a range of short stories with 'beat the monster' as the underlying theme
- Respond and explore purpose and audience for each
- Explore likes, dislikes, puzzles, patterns for each
- Reread parts of Chapter 5 – 'The Iron Man's challenge' – and analyse the structure of this 'beat the monster' story
- Write a simple, model version of *The Iron Man versus The Space Being* story and shared read
- Check that children are clear about 'suspense' – explore this in your model: What happens? How is it portrayed? Language used around 'good' character and 'monster'?
- Collect effective vocabulary and language; build writer's hints

Phase 1 outcome
To know what a good 'beat the monster' story sounds like

PHASE 2

- Hook: photograph of new monster that is threat to the Iron Man
- Use talk activities to explore and imagine what the monster is like: powers, characteristics, etc. Children label their own pictures of the monster and name it
- Further explore plot ideas (1) build-up to the Iron Man beating the monster, (2) the attack itself and (3) how the Iron Man wins
- Orally rehearse ideas, weaving in vocabulary and language collected in phase 1; begin to create plan
- Use talk activities to think through the opening and ending sections
- Finalise plan

Phase 2 outcome
To have planned my own 'beat the monster' story

PHASE 3

- Mock-up finished story book so children can picture it
- Brief shared write to get children started
- Children independently write the opening and build-up paragraphs
- Mark and follow up on issues before they move onto the problem and resolution parts
- Shared write to support, where necessary
- Children independently write rest of story, including the ending
- Support them to edit and refine story
- Publish, share and evaluate

UNIT PLAN

Theme: *The Iron Man* – Newspaper reports   Lower Key Stage 2

FINAL OUTCOME

Newspaper report on the duel between the Iron Man and the Space Being

PHASE 1

- Hook – great sporting events news reports (film/paper) (e.g. boxing, football derbies, tennis)
- General discussion re: news of this nature – Audience? Purpose? How it is handled; sensationalism
- Shared read similar newspaper reports and respond
- Immerse children in this style of newspaper report so that they internalise the language patterns
- Discuss how stories are handled/portrayed
- Check understanding of purpose and audience of newspaper reports
- Collect list of writer's hints, and appropriate vocabulary
- Chunk newspaper report into sections to check understanding of typical structure

Phase 1 outcome

To know what a good newspaper report looks and sounds like

PHASE 2

- Introduce stimulus by rereading relevant parts of the chapter about the Iron Man fighting the Space Being (or watching scenes from *The Iron Giant*)
- Explore key events through drama/freeze-framing
- Hot-seat characters and other parties to collect and develop ideas
- Begin to plan own report
- Explore headline to use
- Orally rehearse use of journalistic language; record key ideas
- Finalise plan

Phase 2 outcome

To have planned my newspaper report

PHASE 3

- Shared write opening, including headline and use of language
- Independent and guided write openings
- Shared write next parts picking up on issues as report progresses
- Support with concluding paragraph – check it has impact
- Peer evaluate success, then edit
- Publish

Recount
Diary extracts: Bradley, Jeff;
emails: between characters at key moments;
letters between characters; biographies:
Bradley, Jeff, Carla

Description
Character portraits: Bradley,
Jeff, Carla, Mrs Ebbel, Claudia;
descriptions of Bradley written
from different
viewpoints

*There's a Boy
in the Girls'
Bathroom*
by Louis
Sachar

Narrative
Write Jeff's story; write the
prequel; write the sequel; write
Carla's story; change the ending
(e.g. so that Carla doesn't leave);
write the *My Parents Didn't
Steal an Elephant* story

Persuasion
Letters: persuade the school
to keep Carla on as a counsellor;
persuade Jeff to persevere with his
friendship with Bradley; persuade
Mrs Ebbel to get to know Bradley;
magazine articles: on buying,
friendship, why 'it's good
to talk'

UNIT PLAN

Theme: *There's a Boy in the Girls' Bathroom* – Recount (biography)

Upper Key Stage 2

FINAL OUTCOME
To write a Bradley Chaulkers biography

PHASE 1

- Shared read biographies from Marcia Williams' *Three Cheers for Inventors*
- Respond – likes, dislikes, puzzles, patterns; and identify purpose and audience
- General discussion re: biographies – check children understand the purpose and audience
- Immerse the children in short biographies
- Identify use of language, collect and create list of writer's hints
- Chunk a simple biography into sections (opening, childhood paragraph(s), later life paragraph(s), conclusion) so that children understand structure

Phase 1 outcome
To know what a good biography sounds like

PHASE 2

- Hook – create timeline of main events for Bradley, and explain task
- Use drama games to explore Bradley's earlier years: What could have led him to be so miserable? Hate school so much?
- Hot-seat Bradley's mum and sister to find out about his life. Hot-seat Bradley to catch up with him – what is he doing now?
- Use talk activities to decide on extra detail, and orally rehearse ideas
- Use chunks from phase 1 to plan biography
- Orally rehearse use of effective language (collected in phase 1)
- Add to plan

Phase 2 outcome
To have planned my biography

PHASE 3

- Shared write opening
- Independent and guided write openings
- Shared write next parts picking up on issues as biography progresses
- Support with concluding paragraph – check it has impact
- Check that the biography has a sensible chronological order and is interesting to read
- Edit and evaluate
- Publish

UNIT PLAN

Theme: *There's a Boy in the Girls' Bathroom* – Description   Upper Key Stage 2

FINAL OUTCOME
To write two character descriptions

PHASE 1

- Read a range of high-quality character descriptions
- Explore and respond – which do you prefer and why?
- Identify audience and purpose for each description read
- Begin to collect writer's hints
- Identify features
- Explore the use of expanded noun phrases; metaphors, onomatopoeia, alliteration to add detail and effect
- Collect and 'play with' effects so that they are internalised and the effects understood
- Chunk a description into sections to get a feel for structure

Phase 1 outcome
To know what good character descriptions sound like

PHASE 2

- Hook – read extracts from the novel that tell us or give us clues about Bradley Chalkers
- Collect ideas to build up a picture of Bradley – inside and out
- Further develop ideas by playing word and language games to support with finding appropriate noun phrases, metaphors and alliteration
- Orally rehearse – support with development
- Plan and write (see Phase 3)
- Second hook – read extracts that refer to another character (children to choose their second character)
- Support children to plan accurate description, using similar approaches to those used above

Phase 2 outcome
To have planned my own character

PHASE 3

Carry out the following process for both descriptions:

- Model how to use plan to write opening of description
- Children write opening independently
- Mark and either model next part or children proceed with writing the rest of their descriptions independently
- Read descriptions aloud in order to support with editing
- Refine, publish and evaluate

UNIT PLAN

Theme: *There's a Boy in the Girls' Bathroom* – **Persuasion**   Upper Key Stage 2

FINAL OUTCOME
Magazine article – bullying

PHASE 1

- Use *There's a Boy in the Girls' Bathroom* as a way into discussing the characters' different experiences of bullying
- Use talk activities to explore the advice that you would give to the characters
- Task: ask the children to write a factual/persuasive magazine article (for the school website) about bullying
- Shared read a variety of magazine articles, including Web-based texts, on issues that typically effect children
- Respond; compare and contrast; and discuss purpose and audience
- Identify effective use of language and collect; build writers' hints
- Discuss layout of most effective texts

Phase 1 outcome

To know what a good issue-based magazine article looks and sounds like

PHASE 2

- Research interesting facts and figures on bullying
- Use talk activities to explore the facts and how best to present them in an article
- Check children are clear about purpose and audience for article
- Begin to plan new article
- Practise using elements from the writer's hints as part of the arguments
- Orally rehearse each section of the article; add vocabulary to plan
- Discuss layout decisions and finalise plan

Phase 2 outcome

To have planned my own magazine article

PHASE 3

- Shared write opening of article – model how to use plan
- Children independently draft the opening
- Shared write to support with main body and closing
- Children independently draft rest of article
- Support them to edit and refine whole text
- Publish polished text together with other design elements
- Share and evaluate

Information
Life on the dumpsite; life for children living on dumpsites; child labour; Third World issues; about projects such as the Small Steps Project; recycling; landfill

Description
Characters: Raphael; Gardo; Rat; Jose; settings: the dump; different parts of the dump; Sampalo; Central Station; police station

Trash
by Andy Mulligan

Narrative
Alternative ending; change what was found – write a short story; write a new adventure for the three characters (fishing related)

Persuasion
Argument: children should never live on dumpsites; it is always wrong to work against 'the law'; join the Small Steps Project campaign; recycling; against landfill

UNIT PLAN

Theme: *Trash* – Setting description   Upper Key Stage 2

FINAL OUTCOME
To write two contrasting setting descriptions

PHASE 1

- Shared read variety of good-quality setting descriptions
- Collect writer's hints
- Play word/language games to develop the language of description (use short film clips as stimulus)
- Explore the use of expanded noun phrases; metaphors, onomatopoeia, alliteration to add detail and effect
- Collect vocabulary and language
- Chunk a setting description into parts so that children understand structure
- Hook – having read *Trash*, collect ideas about the different settings featured

Phase 1 outcome
To know what a good setting description sounds like

PHASE 2

- Explain task – to write two contrasting setting descriptions, one about the dumpsite and one about paradise island
- Begin with the dumpsite – use extracts from the text and photographs games to build a picture of the setting; label with vocabulary; build a bank
- Support the children to create a plan for the setting description
- Introduce stimulus for contrasting setting; use senses to orally build a description; play talk games to develop ideas
- Create a plan for the second setting
- Support children to orally rehearse and refine their descriptions
- Refine contrasting language/vocabulary across the two plans

Phase 2 outcome
To have planned my setting descriptions

PHASE 3

- For dumpsite setting: model write first couple of lines (including modelling how to work from a plan)
- Children independently write their descriptions
- Share and refine
- Children independently write the second descriptions (putting into practice what they have learned from first setting descriptions)
- Edit, refine and publish
- Evaluate

UNIT PLAN

Theme: *Trash* – Information   Upper Key Stage 2

FINAL OUTCOME
Non-chronological report on dumpsite children

PHASE 1

- Shared read a variety of non-chronological reports
- Compare and contrast; explore and respond – likes, dislikes, puzzles, patterns; and identify purpose and audience of each
- Collect writer's hints
- Immerse children in non-chronological reports so that they internalise language structures
- Chunk a text into sections to establish the structure of a report
- Identify key features to add to writer's hints and collect language
- Play word and language games to practise and develop 'report' type vocabulary and structures
- Introduce task: to write a report on dumpsite children

Phase 1 outcome
To know what a good non-chronological report looks and sounds like

PHASE 2

- Establish what children know about dumpsite children
- Support children to research the topic using a variety of sources (film, Internet, etc.); keep it focused (e.g. where in the world, what they do)
- Support children to create new plan: introduction; orally rehearse/discuss what might be in the introduction
- Support children to develop new plan: four key sections; orally rehearse/discuss content of each section (using aspects from writer's hints list to make sure that it's as effective as possible)
- Support children to think about how you might conclude the text; orally rehearse ideas; add these to plan

Phase 2 outcome
To have planned my non-chronological report

PHASE 3

- Shared write intro paragraph
- Children independently write introductory paragraph
- Edit and refine
- In turn, shared write, children independently write, edit and refine next four sections
- Shared/independently write conclusion
- Refine to check for impact on reader
- Share with audience and evaluate

UNIT PLAN

Theme: *Trash* – **Persuasion**   Upper Key Stage 2

FINAL OUTCOME
Campaign leaflet for joining the Small Steps Project

PHASE 1

- Read *Trash*; discuss what children know and understand about dumpsite children
- Check understanding of 'campaign'. Discuss different campaign methods, including leafleting the public
- Shared read a range of campaign leaflets
- Immerse the children in campaign leaflets so that they know some of the typical language structures by heart
- Collect writer's hints and add to list of language/vocabulary collected earlier
- Play language games to practise using persuasive and emotive language
- Discuss layout of most effective leaflets

Phase 1 outcome
To know what a good campaign leaflet looks and sounds like

PHASE 2

- Research the Small Steps Project
- Use talk activities to explore the facts about dumpsite children and how best to present the arguments in a campaign
- Group ideas into themes and generate persuasive sentences – orally rehearse to check that they sound right and have the right effect
- Practise using elements of writer's hints as part of the arguments
- Orally rehearse each section of the leaflet
- Discuss layout decisions and finalise plan

Phase 2 outcome
To have planned my own leaflet

PHASE 3

- Shared write opening of leaflet – model how to use plan
- Children independently draft the opening
- Shared write to support with main body and closing
- Children independently draft rest of leaflet
- Support them to edit and refine whole text
- Publish polished text together with other design elements
- Share and evaluate

Recount
Diaries: Joe's before and after the birthday party; Dicky's before and after the birthday party; letters: Joe to Dicky; Dicky to Joe; Joe to Great Grandmother and vice versa

Description
Characters: Dicky Hutt, Joe, Great Grandmother; settings: the house, Great Grandmother's room; what's behind the door

Who's Afraid?
by Philippa Pearce

Narrative
Write a prequel; new *Who's Afraid?* story with Dicky Hutt or Great Grandmother or Joe's father as the protagonist; new viewpoint: Dicky's story or Great Grandmother's story; new *Who's Afraid?* story

Instructions
How to play . . . hide and seek and other house/garden games; how to defeat Dicky Hutt; Great Grandmother's guide to . . .; Dicky Hutt's recipe for terrorising Joe

UNIT PLAN

Theme: *Who's Afraid?* – Description   Upper Key Stage 2

FINAL OUTCOME

To write two contrasting setting descriptions of Great Grandmother's room

PHASE 1

- Shared read variety of good-quality setting descriptions
- Immerse children in setting descriptions so that they know the language structures by heart
- Collect writer's hints
- Play word/language games to develop the language of description – explore the use of expanded noun phrases; metaphors, onomatopoeia, alliteration to add detail and effect
- Collect vocabulary and language
- Chunk a setting description into parts so that children understand structure

Phase 1 outcome

To know what good setting descriptions sound like

PHASE 2

- Hook – read *Who's Afraid?* up to end of page 3, 'forbidden door'
- Shared read variety of good-quality setting descriptions
- Immerse children in setting descriptions so that they know the language
- Use talk activities to support children to imagine what the room behind the door may look like
- Further develop ideas by playing word and language games to support with finding appropriate noun phrases, metaphors, onomatopoeia and alliteration
- Orally rehearse – support with development
- Plan and write (see Phase 3)
- Second hook – read rest of *Who's Afraid?*
- Support children to plan accurate description of Great Grandmother's room, using similar approaches to those used above

Phase 2 outcome

To have planned my own setting descriptions

PHASE 3

Carry out the following process for both descriptions:

- Model how to use plan to write opening of description
- Children write opening independently
- Mark and either model next part or children proceed with writing the rest of their descriptions independently
- Read descriptions aloud in order to support with editing
- Refine, publish and evaluate

UNIT PLAN

Theme: *Who's Afraid?* – Information   Upper Key Stage 2

FINAL OUTCOME
To write a set of instructions

PHASE 1

- Hook – read *Who's Afraid?* and respond
- Explain task – to make up, and then write a set of instructions for how to defeat Dicky Hutt
- Shared read various sets of instructions; respond; compare and contrast
- Identify the features and typical language of instructions (e.g. introduction, what you need, what you do, bossy verbs, ordered steps, concluding statement)
- Collect writer's hints for instructions
- Play language games to develop understanding of bossy verb meanings (e.g. mime the action)
- Chunk text into sections and discuss layout (purpose)

Phase 1 outcome

To know what a good set of instructions looks and sounds like

PHASE 2

- Reread key moments in *Who's Afraid?* and use drama and freeze-framing to think through what might be good advice for defeating Dicky at each moment
- Using the 'what you do' section as a starting point for planning, begin to orally rehearse and then plan each step
- Add detail to each step (e.g. 'When you hear Dicky's footsteps, be sure to . . .')
- Use talk activities/drama to support with ideas for what you might put into the 'what you need' section (e.g. a haunted house, a Great Grandmother); add to plan
- Use talk activities to support with ideas for an introduction and concluding statement
- Complete plan

Phase 2 outcome

To have planned my instructions

PHASE 3

- Shared write introduction
- Children write introduction and 'what you need' independently
- Shared write initial steps
- Children write steps independently
- Shared write concluding statement
- Children complete independently
- Mark, feed back and edit
- Publish, share and evaluate

UNIT PLAN

Theme: *Who's Afraid?* – Recount (letter)   Upper Key Stage 2

FINAL OUTCOME
To write a letter to
Dicky Hutt, from Joe

PHASE 1

- Hook – *Who's Afraid?* and respond (likes, dislikes, puzzles, patterns)
- Explain task
- Shared read a model letter from one character to another (similar to Joe/Dicky relationship)
- Identify purpose and discuss
- Build a list of writer's hints for letters of this type (avoid an overemphasis on 'informal language')
- Chunk the model letter into parts to support with structure
- Recap layout of letters

Phase 1 outcome
To know what a good
letter sounds like

PHASE 2

- Reread key moments in *Who's Afraid?* and use drama and freeze-framing to support children to think through how Joe was feeling, and what he might want to say to Dicky after the event (including Great Grandmother's subsequent death)
- Start to plan letter
- Play word/language games to orally rehearse the effective use of vocabulary to add detail and make it emotive without being aggressive – children add new ideas to their plan
- Orally rehearse ideas, being careful to weave in writer's hints elements
- Finalise plan

Phase 2 outcome
To have planned my
letter

PHASE 3

- Shared write opening of letter – model how to use plan
- Children independently write the opening
- Mark and follow up on issues before they move onto the main body of the letter
- Shared write to support with main body and closing
- Children independently write rest of letter
- Support them to edit and refine whole text
- Publish, share and evaluate

CHAPTER 3

Using short films as hooks

Mind maps
and unit plans

Recount
What happened when you blew the bubbles (girl 1 and girl 2); postcard from girl 2 to girl 1 telling her what happened; diary entries

Description
Settings; character's feelings; bubbles – what they look like and how they move; new object (e.g. sea shell, key)

Bubbles

available at: https://vimeo.com/21510156

Narrative
Write the story of the film; write a sequel (what happens to the next girl?); invent a new story – a new object with a new transformation/journey

Poetry
Possible themes: feelings, imaginary worlds, bubbles, blowing bubbles, floating/flying/travelling

UNIT PLAN

Theme: *Bubbles* – Narrative   Key Stage 1

FINAL OUTCOME
To write a story based on *Bubbles*

PHASE 1

- Watch *Bubbles* and respond (likes, dislikes, puzzles, patterns)
- Shared read stories with similar plot patterns
- Explore and respond – likes, dislikes, puzzles, patterns
- Collect writer's hints for these stories
- Use a map or storyboard to chart the plot of *Bubbles*
- Use drama/role play to understand the key parts of the plot
- Practise using typical story language to retell the *Bubbles* story

Phase 1 outcome
To know the plot and narrative language in the *Bubbles* story and be able to retell it

PHASE 2

- Use picture or artefact stimulus to discuss other adventures that could be had (similar to *Bubbles*)
- Use drama/role play to explore new adventures: Where would it lead? What would happen?
- Collect vocabulary along the way
- Replace 'bubbles' on story map/board with new idea, or create plan (if ready)
- Replace other elements that will change
- Develop story map/board or plan
- Use word/language games to explore new vocabulary
- Orally rehearse new ideas
- Finalise plan

Phase 2 outcome
To have planned my own alternative *Bubbles* story

PHASE 3

- Show children mock-up of final book
- Model write opening – using story map/plan
- Children write opening independently
- Model write main events – using story map/plan
- Children write main events independently
- Model write ending – using story map/plan
- Children write ending independently
- Mark, feed back and edit
- Publish and share

UNIT PLAN

Theme: *Bubbles* – Poetry   Key Stage 1

PHASE 1

- Read a range of list simile poems (e.g. bubbles poem at www.readwritethink.org)
- Explore and respond – which do you prefer and why?
- Learn a simile list poem by heart
- Use picture stimulus to explore similes
- Begin to collect items for writer's hints
- Expand vocabulary by generating synonyms for colours and size (e.g. 'emerald' instead of 'green'; 'tiny' instead of 'small') and for movement (e.g. floating, gliding)
- Continually read simile poems to develop 'ear' for them, and to add items to writer's hints

Phase 1 outcome
To know what good themed poems are and to be able to retell/perform one

PHASE 2

- Watch *Bubbles*, asking children to focus on the bubbles
- Collect key vocabulary (use photographs of bubbles to add to this)
- Play word and language games to develop ideas around relevant similes
- Plan poem
- Orally rehearse ideas
- Refine and/or develop them

Phase 2 outcome
To have planned my own bubbles poem

PHASE 3

- Model how to use plan to write beginning of poem
- Recap expectations around adventurous vocabulary and use of similes
- Independent write of poems
- Publish poems
- Practise performing poems
- Share and perform poems (use photo montage or *Bubbles* film as visual background)
- Evaluate them

UNIT PLAN

Theme: **Bubbles** – Postcards   Key Stage 1

FINAL OUTCOME
To write postcards to
and from Bubble girls

PHASE 1

- Hook – watch *Bubbles* and read postcard from girl 1 asking girl 2 about whether the bubbles cheered her up
- Discussion about how the class could respond
- Read selection of postcards
- Discuss various purposes/audiences
- Build list of writer's hints for postcards
- Use engaging stimuli to practise writing short, concise messages (bear purpose and audience in mind)

Phase 1 outcome
To know what postcards
are and how they are
used to send short
messages

PHASE 2

- Use drama to explore what girl 2 might have done once she found the bubbles: What do you think happened to her? Where did she go? What did she see?
- Orally rehearse how she might capture these ideas in a postcard
- Create a map or plan
- Orally rehearse then refine plan

Phase 2 outcome
To have planned my
postcards to and from
the Bubble girls

PHASE 3

- Shared write postcard modelling how to use the plan
- Children independently write postcards
- Revise and edit the postcards
- Follow aspects of phase 2 to rehearse and plan postcard to respond
- Shared and independently write second postcard
- Polish and publish

Recount
What happened when you collected the objects; invent new objects/events and recount what happened when you collected them; news reports

Description
Objects inside/outside the bag (e.g. feathers and then birds); invent a new container for the objects and describe

The Girl with the Yellow Bag

available at:
https://vimeo.com/26261136

Narrative
Write the story of the film; add new objects to the story; invent a new story with a new container (e.g. sack, suitcase)

Explanation
How the magic bag works; invent a new container; how the magic . . . works

UNIT PLAN

Theme: *The Girl with the Yellow Bag* – Explanation   Key Stage 1

FINAL OUTCOME

To write an explanation based on *The Girl with the Yellow Bag*

PHASE 1

- Play talk games to establish what an explanation is
- Shared read simple explanations
- Explore and respond – likes, dislikes, puzzles, patterns; and identify audience and purpose of each
- Immerse children in explanation texts, begin to collect writer's hints
- Unpick language features and add key ones to writer's hints
- Identify layout features e.g. diagrams, bullets, headings and purpose of each
- Hook – watch *The Girl with the Yellow Bag* and respond (likes, dislikes, puzzles, patterns)

Phase 1 outcome

To know what a good explanation looks and sounds like

PHASE 2

- Children generate questions about the film e.g. Where is the bag from? Is the girl magic?
- Play explanation talk games to make up answers to the questions
- Choose a question and support with adapting the model text map to plan a new explanation
- Use drama/role play to explore the ideas and language needed for the new explanation)
- Support children to complete a plan
- Play word/language games to orally rehearse the language of explanation

Phase 2 outcome

To have planned my explanation

PHASE 3

- Show children a mock-up of final explanation (i.e. how it could be laid out on the page)
- Shared write opening of explanation – model how to use plan
- Children independently write the opening
- Mark and follow up on issues before they move onto the main body of the explanation
- Shared write to support with main body and closing
- Children independently write rest of explanation
- Add additional elements (e.g. headings, diagrams)
- Support them to edit and refine whole text
- Publish, share and evaluate

UNIT PLAN

Theme: *The Girl with the Yellow Bag* – **Narrative**   Key Stage 1

FINAL OUTCOME

To add to the story based on *The Girl with the Yellow Bag*

PHASE 1

- Hook – watch *The Girl with the Yellow Bag* and respond (likes, dislikes, puzzles, patterns)
- Use a map or storyboard to chart the plot/key events of *The Girl with the Yellow Bag* story
- Use drama/role play to understand the key parts of the plot
- Write model *The Girl with the Yellow Bag* text and shared read
- Focus on the detail of each event (e.g. colourful sock becoming beautiful rainbow, single white feather becoming a flock of snowy doves)
- Collect effective language and vocabulary
- Collect list of ideas for writer's hints – tricks to make the story effective

Phase 1 outcome

To know the key events in *The Girl with the Yellow Bag* story

PHASE 2

- Use artefacts to discuss other objects she might put into her bag and what they might turn into
- Play word/language games to develop ideas and to add detail (as in phase 1)
- Collect vocabulary along the way
- Add new objects and what they turn into to the model map
- Orally rehearse new ideas and add to map or storyboard created in phase 1
- Support children to complete plan

Phase 2 outcome

To have planned my own new events to add to *The Girl with the Yellow Bag* story

PHASE 3

- Shared write new event/object
- Children independently write their first new event
- Shared write how to link events
- Children independently write the rest of their events
- Mark, feed back and edit
- Add into middle of model text (i.e. beginning and end remain the same)
- Publish and share

UNIT PLAN

Theme: *The Girl with the Yellow Bag* – Recount

Key Stage 1

FINAL OUTCOME

To write a recount of the events in *The Girl with the Yellow Bag*

PHASE 1

- Play talk games to establish what a recount is
- Shared read simple recounts
- Compare and contrast; explore and respond – likes, dislikes, puzzles, patterns; and identify audience and purpose of each
- Write a model recount that is similar to *The Girl with the Yellow Bag*
- Play with the sentence structures and vocabulary in the model so that children are clear about this text type
- Chunk the model into key events – build a bank of vocabulary for each, and develop children's understanding of this vocabulary
- Use the model to support knowledge of structure and explore the use of time connectives
- Collect writer's hints for a recount

Phase 1 outcome

To know what a good recount sounds like

PHASE 2

- Hook – watch *The Girl with the Yellow Bag* and respond (likes, dislikes, puzzles, patterns)
- Sequence and map the main events
- Use freeze-framing to add detail to each event (e.g. colourful sock becoming beautiful rainbow, single white feather becoming a flock of snowy doves)
- Collect vocabulary
- Support children to plan their recount
- Play word/language games to orally rehearse the use of time words – children add these to their plan
- Finalise plan

Phase 2 outcome

To have planned my recount

PHASE 3

- Shared write opening of recount – model how to use plan
- Children independently write the opening
- Mark and follow up on issues before they move onto the main body of the recount
- Shared write to support with main body and closing
- Children independently write rest of recount
- Support them to edit and refine whole text
- Publish, share and evaluate

Explanation
How did the turtles come
to be in the sky? How do boats fly?
Why sea turtles are important
(ecology/tourism/culture)?

Description
Fantasy settings; sky/cloud
settings; floating, flying; turtles
swimming (flying); other
animals flying

*Once in a
Lifetime*

available at:
https://vimeo.com/
23805703

Narrative
Write the story of the film;
write a prequel (Who is the man?
How does he get there? Where have
the turtles come from?); write a
sequel to the film; invent a new
story with new animals

Recount
News reports: flying boat;
man travels on turtle's back; man's
journey/diary; turtle's journey/
diary; eyewitness report

Information
Turtle (or other animal) fact file;
report about animal conservation
(e.g. WWF)

UNIT PLAN

Theme: *Once in a Lifetime* – Setting description   Key Stage 1/Year 3

FINAL OUTCOME
To write a setting description

PHASE 1

- Shared read known stories and use them to discuss what 'settings' are
- Shared read and immerse children in a variety of good-quality setting descriptions
- Collect list of writer's hints for setting descriptions
- Play word/language games to develop the language of description
- Chunk a setting description into parts so that children understand structure
- Play barrier game – teacher describes a familiar setting, children draw and compare; do in pairs

Phase 1 outcome

To know what a good setting description sounds like

PHASE 2

- Hook – watch *Once in a Lifetime*
- Use stills from this, and other 'sky/clouds' picture stimulus to generate ideas and vocabulary for the sky setting
- Support the children to create a plan for the setting description (e.g. journey from one side to the other or from bottom to top)
- Pair work – children 'talk' their descriptions (use adventurous vocabulary and similes if possible)
- Play word/language games to continue to develop and rehearse the language of description

Phase 2 outcome

To have planned my setting description

PHASE 3

- Model write first couple of lines
- Children independently write their descriptions
- Share and refine
- Publish by performing them with film stills/pictures as a backdrop and sky/clouds music or percussion accompaniment

UNIT PLAN

Theme: *Once in a Lifetime* – **Explanation**   Key Stage 1/Year 3

FINAL OUTCOME

To write an explanation based on *Once in a Lifetime*

PHASE 1

- Play talk games to establish what an explanation is (e.g. explain how you got to school this morning, explain why the sky is blue)
- Shared read simple explanations
- Explore and respond – likes, dislikes, puzzles, patterns; and identify audience and purpose of each
- Immerse children in explanation texts, begin to collect writer's hints
- Unpick language features and add key ones to writer's hints
- Identify layout features (e.g. diagrams, bullets, headings and purpose of each)
- Watch *Once in a Lifetime* and respond (likes, dislikes, puzzles, patterns)

Phase 1 outcome

To know what a good explanation looks and sounds like

PHASE 2

- Children generate questions about the film (e.g. Where is the man going? How did he get there?)
- Play explanation talk games to make up answers to the questions
- Choose one of the questions and support with adapting the model text map to plan a new explanation
- Use drama/role play to explore the ideas and language needed for the new explanation (e.g. How would we explain how boats fly?)
- Support children to complete their plan
- Play word/language games to orally rehearse the language of explanation

Phase 2 outcome

To have planned my explanation

PHASE 3

- Show children a mock-up of final explanation (i.e. how it could be laid out on the page)
- Shared write opening of explanation – model how to use plan
- Children independently write the opening
- Mark and follow up on issues before they move onto the main body of the explanation
- Shared write to support with main body and closing
- Children independently write rest of explanation
- Add additional elements (e.g. headings, diagrams)
- Support them to edit and refine whole text
- Publish, share and evaluate

UNIT PLAN

Theme: *Once in a Lifetime* – Turtle fact file   Key Stage 1/Year 3

FINAL OUTCOME
To write a turtle fact file

PHASE 1

- Read a range of information texts/fact files
- Explore and respond – which do you prefer and why?
- Immerse children in 'reptiles' (e.g. lizards, snakes), fact files
- Collect list of writer's hints
- Identify fact file features
- Collect technical vocabulary
- Short write a fact file on tortoise/crocodile/similar (assess skills/knowledge)
- Address misconceptions

Phase 1 outcome
To know what a good fact file looks and sounds like

PHASE 2

- Hook – watch *Once in a Lifetime*
- Explain task and carry out research activity into turtles
- Explore key information and record vocabulary
- Play word and language games to develop ideas and practise using vocabulary
- Map and plan turtle fact file (including 'design' decisions)
- Orally rehearse ideas
- Refine and/or develop them

Phase 2 outcome
To have planned my fact file

PHASE 3

- Model how to use plan to write fact file introduction, and shared write
- Independent write of introductions
- Model how to use plan to write next part of fact file, and shared write
- Independent write of next parts
- Redraft elements that need polishing
- Publish

Instructions
How to swim in a washing machine;
how to [swim/fly/walk/etc.]
in a(n) [everyday object]

Description
Describe the inside of the
machine; create new characters and
describe them; invent and describe
a new fantasy world inside an
everyday object

Something Fishy

available at:
https://vimeo.com/
24962214

Narrative
Write the story of the film;
write a sequel to the film; change
what she sees when she's in the
washing machine – invent a new story;
invent a new story using a
different everyday object as
a trigger

Poetry
Imaginary worlds;
swimming/flying/etc.;
personification: 'If a pair of
jeans were a shark . . .'

UNIT PLAN

Theme: *Something Fishy* – Character description   Key Stage 1/Year 3

FINAL OUTCOME
To write character descriptions based on *Something Fishy*

PHASE 1

- Shared read a variety of character descriptions (preferably known characters such as the Gruffalo, Big Bad Wolf, etc.)
- Compare and contrast – which are effective and why?
- Hook – watch *Something Fishy*
- Write a model character description (of the shark from *Something Fishy* – physical features and characteristics) and shared read
- Collect writer's hints
- Collect descriptive language and vocabulary

Phase 1 outcome
To know what a good character description sounds like

PHASE 2

- Use stills from *Something Fishy* to generate ideas and vocabulary for the sock-fish, hat-turtles, or t-shirt-octopus
- Play word/language games to develop the language of description
- Use 'laundry items' to come up with new characters for the film (e.g. skirt-jellyfish)
- Use role play to support the children with ideas for the character description – physical description and characteristics, and create a plan
- Pair work – children 'talk' their descriptions
- Play word/language games to continue to develop and rehearse the language of description
- Finalise plans

Phase 2 outcome
To have planned my character descriptions

PHASE 3

- Model write first couple of lines
- Children independently write their descriptions
- Refine
- Publish

UNIT PLAN

Theme: *Something Fishy* – Instructions

Key Stage 1/Year 3

FINAL OUTCOME
To write a set of instructions

PHASE 1

- Hook – watch *Something Fishy*
- Explain task – to write a set of instructions for how to swim in a washing machine
- Shared read various sets of instructions
- Explore and respond – compare and contrast
- Identify the features and typical language of instructions
- Write a model set of instructions (must be similar to 'how to swim in a washing machine'), and shared read
- Build list of writer's hints for instructions
- Play language games to develop understanding of bossy verb meanings (e.g. mime the action)
- Chunk text into sections and discuss layout (purpose)

Phase 1 outcome
To know what a good set of instructions looks and sounds like

PHASE 2

- Play games that involve the children giving instructions to each other
- Watch *Something Fishy* again and use drama/role play to explore the instructions you might give for someone who wants to swim in a washing machine
- Use chunks from phase 1 to begin to plan new set of instructions
- Practise use of bossy verbs appropriate to this set of instructions
- Talk activities to support with ideas for what you might put into an introduction, and the 'what you need' section
- Talk activities to support with ideas for adding detail into each step (e.g. hide yourself among the fish in case a shark comes)
- Support with ideas for a concluding statement
- Complete plan

Phase 2 outcome
To have planned my instructions

PHASE 3

- Shared write introduction
- Children write introduction and 'what you need' independently
- Shared write initial steps
- Children write steps independently
- Shared write concluding statement
- Children complete independently
- Mark, feed back and edit
- Publish and share (could 'perform' them with film running in the background and watery music or percussion accompaniment)

UNIT PLAN

Theme: *Something Fishy* – **Narrative**   Key Stage 1/Year 3

FINAL OUTCOME
To write the story of the film *Something Fishy*

PHASE 1

- Shared read, watch film shorts, or retell a variety of known stories; support children to identify the parts of each story (i.e. opening, build-up, problem, resolution, ending)
- Play story-making games to consolidate understanding of plot
- Use map or storyboard to chart the plot of a simple story of a film – focus on how the parts link and flow (e.g. use of time words or signposts 'suddenly', 'unfortunately')
- Hook – watch *Something Fishy*
- Identify the five parts of the story and what happens in each part
- Explain task – to write the story of the film

Phase 1 outcome

To know what plot is and how the parts of a story flow from start to end

PHASE 2

- Support children to create a story map or storyboard of *Something Fishy*
- Use drama to orally rehearse each key event and add detail (e.g. thoughts and feelings, descriptions of the characters and setting)
- Use word/language games to explore key vocabulary, especially links between events and signposts
- Add to maps or storyboards so that children have a coherent and detailed plan

Phase 2 outcome

To have planned my *Something Fishy* story

PHASE 3

- Show children a mock-up of final book or format for publishing stories
- Shared write story opening
- Children write opening independently
- Shared write build-up
- Children write build-up independently
- Shared write problem and resolution
- Children write problem and resolution independently
- Shared write ending
- Children write ending independently
- Polish
- Publish, illustrate and share

Recount
News reports; interviews with eyewitnesses (drivers); eyewitness reports; first-person accounts (dog 1 and dog 2); dog owners' accounts)

Description
Settings: soundscapes of first two frames; road scene; final frame; characters: two dogs

Stray
available at: www.youtube.com/watch?v=_lOlirEuP_8

Narrative
Write the story of the film; write dialogue for the key moments in the story; change the setting; change the animal

Instructions
Road safety; caring for people who are sick; caring for pets

Persuasion
Letters in support of reducing strays; 'dogs are for life . . .' posters/adverts; road safety posters/adverts

UNIT PLAN

Theme: *Stray* – Narrative (dialogue)   Key Stage 1

FINAL OUTCOME
To write dialogue based on *Stray*

PHASE 1

- Look at stills or pictures from key moments in well-known stories or films and ask children to tell you (guess) what the people are saying
- Write down some of the dialogue – use speech bubbles or similar
- Explain the term 'dialogue' and play talk games that involve the children inventing (or retelling) dialogue
- Using the original stills or pictures focus on what the dialogue tells us about the characters who are speaking. Now do the same activity but without visual images – listening to dialogue – what do we learn about characters?
- Support children with 'feelings' vocabulary (e.g. upset, angry, worried, jealous)

Phase 1 outcome

To know what dialogue is and how it is used to tell us more about characters in stories

PHASE 2

- Hook – watch *Stray*
- Freeze-frame and use role play to imagine what the characters (mainly dogs but could introduce car drivers, etc.) might be saying
- Develop this so that what they are saying is telling us something about how the characters are feeling
- Do this for several different scenes from *Stray*

Phase 2 outcome

To have planned my dialogue

PHASE 3

- Using stills from the film as stimulus, and speech bubbles, shared write dialogue
- Children use stills and speech bubbles to independently write dialogue
- Polish
- Publish (could be recorded and played 'over' the film)

UNIT PLAN

Theme: *Stray* – Newspaper reports   Key Stage 1

FINAL OUTCOME
Newspaper report based on the events of *Stray*

PHASE 1

- Hook – watch simple news reports (e.g. Newsround)
- General discussion re: news – What does it mean? Why do we need it?
- Talk activities to explore what our 'news' is
- Shared read age-appropriate newspaper reports and respond
- Immerse children in newspaper reports so that they internalise the language patterns
- Discuss how stories are handled/portrayed
- Check understanding of purpose and audience of newspaper reports
- Collect list of writer's hints, and appropriate vocabulary
- Chunk newspaper report into sections to check understanding of typical structure (headline, '5 W's intro para, story para, background/eyewitness para, concluding para)

Phase 1 outcome

To know what a good newspaper report looks and sounds like

PHASE 2

- Watch *Stray* to introduce stimulus for newspaper reports
- Map then explore key events through drama/freeze-framing and hot-seating
- Use chunks from phase 1 to support with planning *Stray* report
- Explore headline to use
- Orally rehearse use of journalistic language – weave through key events from *Stray*
- Hot-seat 'witnesses' to get quotes for report
- Orally rehearse concluding statements
- Finalise plan

Phase 2 outcome

To have planned my newspaper report

PHASE 3

- Shared write opening, including headline and use of language
- Independent and guided write openings
- Shared write next parts picking up on issues as report progresses
- Peer evaluate success, then edit
- Publish

UNIT PLAN

Theme: *Stray* – **Persuasion**   Key Stage 1

FINAL OUTCOME
Persuasive poster
based on *Stray*

PHASE 1

- Hook – watch TV adverts around a theme (e.g. toys, cars)
- General discussion re: adverts – purpose and audience?
- Look at and discuss information/persuasive posters (e.g. smoking campaigns, charity campaigns)
- Discuss purpose and audience; compare and contrast
- Learn the text from a simple persuasive poster to internalise language
- Collect effective vocabulary and language structures
- Discuss any relevant design features (which children may use on their own posters)

Phase 1 outcome

To know what persuasion is and what a good persuasive poster looks and sounds like

PHASE 2

- Watch *Stray* to introduce stimulus for persuasive posters
- Introduce facts and interesting information about stray dogs – help children to understand the issues associated with strays (e.g. zone of relevance activity)
- Use drama to help children explore what they might say to persuade someone to keep their dog and look after it properly
- Introduce the vocabulary collected at phase 1 – orally rehearse using this as part of the persuasion
- Support children to decide on the key theme of their posters

Phase 2 outcome

To have planned my persuasive poster

PHASE 3

- Shared write the poster
- Independent and guided write posters
- Share, evaluate and redraft to ensure message is clear
- Make final design decisions (e.g. size of text; page layout; inclusion of photographs, etc.)
- Publish and evaluate for overall impact of poster

Explanation
How does clockwork work?
Why does the world stop when the
dancer stops? Invent your own
and explain it

Description
Contrasting descriptions:
the dancer inside the clock tower
and outside; the settings when she's
inside and outside; invent
another character

The Clocktower

available at:
www.youtube.com/
watch?v=nMlOuP
xhCVI

Narrative
Write the story of the film;
write a prequel (how does she end
up in the clock tower?); write a sequel
to the film; write a story from the
point of view of someone who
lives in the town

Poetry
Possible themes:
feelings, dancing, clocks, clockwork,
darkness, imaginary
worlds

Discussion
Should the dancer stay
in the clock tower? Are the
balloons important to the
ecology of the town?

UNIT PLAN

Theme: *The Clocktower* – Discussion   Key Stage 1/Year 3

FINAL OUTCOME

To write a discussion based on *The Clocktower*

PHASE 1

- Shared read a range of age-appropriate discussion texts
- Use talk activities to further explore 'discussion', including purpose and audience
- Immerse children in simple discussion texts so that they have internalised the language; check understanding of typical language and collect writer's hints
- Play language games to practise using simple discursive language and understand what makes it effective
- Chunk simple text into sections (introduction, points for, points against, conclusion); and discuss layout (NB: This is easier for children if the title is expressed as a question, e.g. Should children wear school uniform?)
- Hook – watch *The Clocktower* and respond (likes, dislikes, puzzles, patterns)

Phase 1 outcome

To know what a good discussion looks and sounds like

PHASE 2

- Discuss whether the dancer should stay in the clock tower: What would happen if the dancer left? How would it affect the town?
- Task: to write a discussion – should the dancer leave?
- Hot-seat the dancer and people from the town
- Support the children to understand the reasons why she should and shouldn't leave; play language games to expand these arguments
- Support children to plan their discussion using chunks from phase 1
- Orally rehearse opening and closing: check for impact
- Finalise plan

Phase 2 outcome

To have planned my discussion

PHASE 3

- Shared write opening of discussion – model how to use plan
- Children independently write the opening
- Shared write to support with 'reasons for' section
- Children independently write 'reasons for' section
- Shared write to support with 'reasons against' section
- Children independently write 'reasons against' section
- Shared/independently write conclusion
- Edit and refine
- Publish, share and evaluate (you could invite an audience to watch the film and then listen to the class's discussion)

UNIT PLAN

Theme: *The Clocktower* – Explanation   Key Stage 1/Year 3

FINAL OUTCOME
To write an explanation based on *The Clocktower*

PHASE 1

- Play talk games to establish what an explanation is
- Shared read simple explanations
- Explore and respond – likes, dislikes, puzzles, patterns; and identify audience and purpose of each
- Immerse children in explanation texts, begin to collect writer's hints
- Unpick language features and add key ones to writer's hints
- Identify layout features (e.g. diagrams, bullets, headings and purpose of each)
- Hook – watch *The Clocktower* and respond (likes, dislikes, puzzles, patterns)

Phase 1 outcome
To know what a good explanation looks and sounds like

PHASE 2

- Children generate questions about the film (e.g. Why is the dancer there? Who lives in the town?)
- Make up answers to the questions through talk games
- Choose one of the above questions and support with adapting the model text map to plan a new explanation
- Use drama/role play to explore the ideas and language needed for the new explanation (e.g. How would we explain why she is there?)
- Support children to complete their plan
- Play word/language games to orally rehearse the language of explanation

Phase 2 outcome
To have planned my explanation

PHASE 3

- Show children a mock-up of final explanation (i.e. how it could be laid out on the page)
- Shared write opening of explanation – model how to use plan
- Children independently write the opening
- Mark and follow up on issues before they move onto the main body of the explanation
- Shared write to support with main body and closing
- Children independently write rest of explanation
- Add additional elements (e.g. headings, diagrams)
- Support them to edit and refine whole text
- Publish, share and evaluate

UNIT PLAN

Theme: *The Clocktower* – **Narrative**   Key Stage 1/Year 3

FINAL OUTCOME

To write a prequel to
The Clocktower

PHASE 1

- Read a range of short stories with good versus evil as the underlying theme – traditional tales such as *Cinderella* and *Snow White* are good for this
- Explore likes, dislikes, puzzles, patterns for each
- Reread and discuss how you might make each story have a sad (as opposed to happy) ending
- Use drama/role play to explore this (try to make the 'good' character lose out each time)
- Collect vocabulary that helps to build a sad, sympathetic effect
- Use mapping or a story mountain to identify typical plot structure to these types of stories (i.e. opening, build-up, problem, resolution, ending)
- Collect list of writer's hints – tools that make a good versus evil story effective?

Phase 1 outcome

To know what a good 'good versus evil' story sounds like

PHASE 2

- Hook – watch *The Clocktower*
- Support children to think how the dancer ended up in the clock tower
- Use drama and role play to guide thinking through the good versus evil story
- Create individual story maps, storyboards or plans
- Orally rehearse main events, making sure that 'mood' vocabulary is used (we need to feel really sorry for the dancer and really dislike the 'evil' character who has put her in the clock tower)
- Finalise plans (or maps/storyboards)

Phase 2 outcome

To have planned my own good versus evil story

PHASE 3

- Show children mock-up of final book
- Model write opening – using story map/plan
- Children write opening independently
- Model write main events – using story map/plan
- Children write main events independently
- Model write ending – using story map/plan
- Children write ending independently
- Mark, feed back and edit
- Publish and share

Recount
A day in the life of the girl; letter/postcard to the girl recounting your typical day; reply from the girl recounting other events in her village; factual about how to get water (when you don't have it on tap)

Description
Settings; compare and contrast to own country/town; character: actions, feelings, dress, physical features

Zahra

available at:
https://vimeo.com/23455377

Narrative
Write the story of the film; change the key event in the story; invent a new story set in the girl's village; invent a new adventure for the girl

Information
Report about: children living in contrasting localities; water issues (e.g. people living without it on tap, unclean, etc.); information on growing things

UNIT PLAN

Theme: *Zahra* – Setting description   Key Stage 1

FINAL OUTCOME
To write contrasting setting descriptions

PHASE 1

- Shared read known stories and use them to discuss what 'settings' are
- Shared read and immerse children in a variety of good-quality setting descriptions
- Collect list of writer's hints for setting descriptions
- Play word/language games to develop the language of description
- Chunk a setting description into parts so that children understand structure
- Play barrier game – teacher describes a familiar setting, children draw and compare; do in pairs

Phase 1 outcome
To know what a good setting description sounds like

PHASE 2

- Shared/independently write a description of their street
- Hook – watch *Zahra*
- Use stills from this, and other desert picture stimulus, to generate ideas and vocabulary for the setting
- Support the children to create a plan for the setting description (e.g. journey from one side to the other or from bottom to top)
- Pair work – children 'talk' their descriptions (use adventurous vocabulary and similes if possible)
- Use talk to address issues from familiar setting description completed at start of phase 2

Phase 2 outcome
To have planned my setting description

PHASE 3

- Model write first couple of lines
- Children independently write their descriptions
- Share and refine
- 'Perform' them with film stills/pictures as a backdrop and the film soundtrack as accompaniment
- Publish alongside the familiar setting descriptions

UNIT PLAN

Theme: *Zahra* – **Information**   Key Stage 1

FINAL OUTCOME
Information text on water issues in Africa

PHASE 1

- Hook – watch *Zahra*
- Establish what children know about water issues in other countries
- Explain task; then shared read a range of information texts
- Explore and respond: Which do you prefer and why? Purpose and audience of each?
- Immerse children in 'issue-based' information texts
- Chunk a simple information text to help to identify information page features
- Collect technical vocabulary
- Collect list of writer's hints

Phase 1 outcome
To know what a good information text looks and sounds like

PHASE 2

- Use a variety of information texts (film, Internet, etc.) to provide content
- Use word and language games to check understanding of technical vocabulary, and of appropriate conjunctions
- Plan introduction; orally rehearse/discuss what might be in the introduction
- Plan two key sections (travelling for water and drinking dirty water and conclusion); orally rehearse/discuss content
- Make design decisions and finalise plan

Phase 2 outcome
To have planned my information text

PHASE 3

- Shared write introductory paragraph
- Children independently write introductory paragraph
- Edit and refine
- In turn, shared write, children independently write, edit and refine next two sections
- Shared/independently write conclusion
- Decide on layout of final text – add pictures etc.
- Refine to check for impact on reader
- Share with audience and evaluate

UNIT PLAN

Theme: *Zahra* – **Recount**   Key Stage 1

FINAL OUTCOME
To write a day in the life of Zahra

PHASE 1

- Play talk games to establish what a recount is (e.g. recount your journey to school, what you did on Sunday)
- Shared read simple recounts
- Compare and contrast; explore and respond – likes, dislikes, puzzles, patterns; and identify audience and purpose of each
- Write a model recount that is similar to a day in the life of Zahra
- Play with the sentence structures and vocabulary in the model so that children are clear about this text type
- Chunk the model into key events – build a bank of vocabulary for each, and develop children's understanding of this vocabulary
- Use the model to support knowledge of structure and explore the use of time connectives
- Collect writer's hints for a recount
- Hook – watch *Zahra* and respond (likes, dislikes, puzzles, patterns)

Phase 1 outcome
To know what a good recount sounds like

PHASE 2

- Support the children to sequence and map the main events from the film
- Use freeze-framing to add detail to each event: How did she feel? The movement of the water, leaves, etc.
- Collect vocabulary
- Support children to plan their recount
- Play word/language games to orally rehearse the use of time words – children add these to their plan
- Play word/language games to orally rehearse the use of vocabulary to add detail
- Finalise plan

Phase 2 outcome
To have planned my recount

PHASE 3

- Shared write opening of recount – model how to use plan
- Children independently write the opening
- Mark and follow up on issues before they move onto the main body of the recount
- Shared write to support with main body and closing
- Children independently write rest of recount
- Support them to edit and refine whole text
- Publish, share and evaluate

Mind maps
and unit plans

Recount
First-person account of events;
diary entry; a different doll's
story; newspaper report about
the shop/events

Description
The shop (inside and outside);
Alma; the dolls

Alma

available at:
www.youtube.com/
watch?v=tECaYQ
1AzkM

Narrative
Write the story of the film;
write a stream of consciousness;
add dialogue; stop the action when
she tries to reach the Alma doll and
write the ending; write the sequel;
change the ending; add a scene
about one of the other dolls
(e.g. man on bike)

Discussion
Do ghosts exist? Do aliens
exist? Can we always explain
everything that happens?

UNIT PLAN

Theme: *Alma* – Discussion

Upper Key Stage 2

FINAL OUTCOME
To write a discussion about whether ghosts exist

PHASE 1

- Read a range of discussion texts
- Explore purpose and audience for each
- Use talk activities to further explore the concept of 'discussion'
- Collect list of writer's hints
- Play language games to practise using discursive language
- Chunk a discursive text into sections to clarify structure of discussion texts (paragraphs: intro, points for, points against, conclusion)

Phase 1 outcome
To know what a good discussion text looks and sounds like

PHASE 2

- Hook – watch *Alma*
- Introduce task: discussion 'do ghosts exist?'; hold an initial class discussion on this
- Children to research reasons that prove/disprove that ghosts exist
- Use chunked text from phase 1 to start to plan new discussion
- Use discussion-based role-play and drama games to explore reasons for and against the existence of ghosts
- Use language games to further explore the effective use of discursive language
- Orally rehearse possible introductions/conclusions to this discussion
- Complete plan

Phase 2 outcome
To have planned my own discussion text

PHASE 3

- Shared write introduction and points for paragraph(s)
- Children independently write introduction and points for paragraph(s)
- Shared write points against and concluding paragraphs
- Children independently write points against and concluding paragraphs
- Support with editing and refining discussions
- Share and evaluate
- Publish

UNIT PLAN

Theme: *Alma* – Narrative

Upper Key Stage 2

FINAL OUTCOME
To predict and write
the ending to *Alma*

PHASE 1

- Watch short spooky films, respond to and analyse endings (likes, dislikes, puzzles, patterns)
- Read a range of short spooky stories; respond to and analyse endings (likes, dislikes, puzzles, patterns)
- Collect language and vocabulary that are effective
- Collect writer's hints – tools/tricks that make an ending really effective
- Use mapping to identify typical pattern of endings

Phase 1 outcome
To know what a good
spooky story ending
looks and sounds like
(plot and language)

PHASE 2

- Hook – watch *Alma* up to the point where she tries to reach the Alma doll
- Support children to think about how the story might end: Does she reach the doll? If so, what happens next? If not, what happens? How do you think it could end?
- Use drama and role play to guide thinking through the main events building to the ending (guide towards spooky/chilling end)
- Begin to plan chosen ending
- Use oral rehearsal and further drama activities to check that the planned ending is going to have the desired impact on the audience
- Support children to plan how they will incorporate vocabulary, language and suspense devices from phase 1

Phase 2 outcome
To have planned my
spooky story ending

PHASE 3

- Shared write the first part of a story ending to get the writing process started
- Children independently write
- Mark and follow up on issues before they move onto completing their endings
- Shared write to support, where necessary
- Support them to edit and refine story ending
- Share and evaluate
- Publish

UNIT PLAN

Theme: *Alma* – **Newspaper report**   Upper Key Stage 2

FINAL OUTCOME
To write a newspaper report based on *Alma*

PHASE 1

- Hook – watch short newsreels or read newspaper articles about spooky/unexplained event
- General discussion re: news of this nature
- Audience? Purpose? How it is handled; sensationalism
- Use map and actions to learn a newspaper report
- Read selection of other, similar, newspaper reports and identify use of language, magpie
- Check understanding of structure of newspaper reports (headline, '5 W's intro para, story para, background/eyewitness para, concluding para)
- Box up learned newspaper report

Phase 1 outcome

To know what a good newspaper report looks and sounds like

PHASE 2

- Introduce stimulus by watching *Alma*
- Discuss the focus and key events that you could report on in a news report and explore through drama/freeze-framing
- Hot-seat characters and other parties to collect and develop ideas (including quotes) for e.g. Alma's family; the girl outside the shop; police investigator
- Box up and plan own report (support children so that the focus of the article is clear, e.g. *Young Girl Narrowly Escapes* or *Spooky Shop Discovered*)
- Explore headline to use
- Orally rehearse use of journalistic language; record key ideas

Phase 2 outcome

To have planned my own newspaper report

PHASE 3

- Shared write opening, including headline and use of language
- Independent and guided write openings
- Shared write next parts picking up on issues as report progresses
- Support with concluding paragraph – check it has impact
- Peer evaluate success, then edit
- Publish

Information
Possible themes: circuses/cirque du soleil; tightrope walking; carnivals; famous traditions; unusual hobbies; information leaflet about El Caminante's tightrope walk

Description
Use the soundtrack and colours, light and shade to help describe the settings; El Caminante; one of the children; one of the adults

El Caminante

(from the *British Film Institute: Story Shorts* DVD)

Narrative
Write the story of the film; stop the action when he is halfway across the tightrope and write the ending; write a sequel (what happens the following year?); write the dialogue for key moments

Recount
Letters or postcards recounting the day's events; series of diary entries before, during, after the event; live commentary of the tightrope walk; El Caminante's biography

UNIT PLAN

Theme: **El Caminante – Recount (biography)**   Key Stage 2

FINAL OUTCOME
El Caminante's biography

PHASE 1

- Shared read biographies from Marcia Williams' *Three Cheers for Inventors*
- Respond – likes, dislikes, puzzles, patterns; and identify purpose and audience
- General discussion re: biographies – check children understand the purpose and audience
- Immerse the children in short biographies
- Identify use of language, collect and create list of writer's hints
- Chunk a simple biography into sections (opening, childhood paragraph(s), later life paragraph(s), conclusion) so that children understand structure

Phase 1 outcome
To know what a good biography sounds like

PHASE 2

- Hook – watch *El Caminante*
- Hot-seat El Caminante (and others, e.g. his mum, best friend, etc.) to find out about his life
- Research life in Andalusia, and the lives of famous tightrope walkers to add extra detail
- Use chunks from phase 1 to plan biography
- Orally rehearse use of effective language (collected in phase 1)
- Add to plan

Phase 2 outcome
To have planned my biography

PHASE 3

- Shared write opening
- Independent and guided write openings
- Shared write next parts picking up on issues as biography progresses
- Support with concluding paragraph – check it has impact
- Check that the biography has a sensible chronological order and is interesting to read
- Edit and evaluate
- Publish

UNIT PLAN

Theme: *El Caminante* – Setting description   Key Stage 2

FINAL OUTCOME
To write three setting descriptions

PHASE 1

- Establish what children know about 'settings' and how to describe them
- Shared read setting descriptions
- Compare and contrast; explore and respond – likes, dislikes, puzzles, patterns; and identify purpose and audience of each
- Immerse children in setting descriptions so that they internalise the language structures
- Collect writer's hints and effective vocabulary
- Play word/language games to develop the language of description
- Chunk a setting description into parts so that children understand structure
- Play word/language games to develop the language of description (use short film clips as stimulus)

Phase 1 outcome
To know what a good setting description sounds like

PHASE 2

- Hook – watch *El Caminante*
- Explain task – to write three setting descriptions, one each from beginning, middle and end of the film
- Use clips from each part to generate ideas and vocabulary (focus on use of light/shade and sound)
- Support the children to plan each setting description
- Pair work – children 'talk' their descriptions
- Play word/language games to continue to develop and rehearse the language of description

Phase 2 outcome
To have planned my setting descriptions

PHASE 3

For each description:

- Model write first couple of lines
- Children independently write their descriptions
- Share and refine
- Publish

UNIT PLAN

Theme: *El Caminante* – Information text   Key Stage 2

FINAL OUTCOME
Non-chronological report about unusual hobbies

PHASE 1

- Hook – watch *El Caminante*, ask children if they know of any other unusual (dangerous) hobbies
- Research unusual hobbies to engage the children in the subject then explain task
- Shared read simple non-chronological reports; compare and contrast; respond and identify purpose and audience
- Immerse children in simple non-chronological reports so that they internalise language structures; collect writer's hints
- Chunk a text into sections to establish the structure of a report
- Identify key features, collect language and add to writer's hints
- Play word and language games to practise and develop 'report' type vocabulary and structures

Phase 1 outcome

To know what a good non-chronological report looks and sounds like

PHASE 2

- Support the children to research a chosen unusual hobby
- Using a model text as a frame, decide on the key paragraphs of the report (use areas that the children have identified)
- Support children to generate their own plan, making sure that there is enough information for each paragraph
- Children 'talk' their paragraph ideas to orally rehearse and refine
- Orally rehearse use of appropriate and effective language
- Use model text to support children to make design decisions: What will their report look like on the page? Are they going to add any pictures? Where will they go? Why?
- Finalise plans

Phase 2 outcome

To have planned my non-chronological report

PHASE 3

- Shared write opening paragraph – model how to use the plan as a guide
- Independent and guided writing opening paragraphs
- Shared write next parts picking up on issues as report progresses
- Support with polishing final draft, including design decisions (add pictures if required)
- Edit and evaluate
- Publish

Information
Themed: animals/creatures on Pandora; vegetation; people from Pandora; Pandora's sister planet; travel writing

Description
Animals/creatures, Pandora environment, people on Pandora

Pandora Discovered

available at: www.youtube.com/watch?v=GBGD min_38E

Narrative
Write a narrative set on Pandora: flashback to early life; flash forward; develop characters from Pandora and their stories; Pandora myths and legends

Explanation
How to care for creatures on Pandora; invent a vehicle for travelling around Pandora and explain how to use it; life cycle of a creature

Persuasion
Travel brochure page for visiting Pandora; argument for/against: living on Pandora; space travel; life on Mars; investment in space exploration

UNIT PLAN

Theme: *Pandora Discovered* – Explanation   Upper Key Stage 2

FINAL OUTCOME

To write an explanation of how to care for creatures on Pandora

PHASE 1

- Shared read explanation texts
- Compare and contrast; explore and respond
- Immerse children in explanation texts so that they internalise the language
- Unpick language features and understand why they are used/effective; build list of writer's hints
- Build word bank of technical vocabulary (short write glossary) and other 'explanation'-type words/phrases
- Check understanding of the structure of the explanation text
- Discuss layout (purpose)

Phase 1 outcome

To know what a good explanation text looks and sounds like

PHASE 2

- Hook – watch *Pandora Discovered* and introduce explanation task
- Use hook and picture/video stimulus to discuss technical vocabulary needed for writing explanation
- Begin to build list of relevant technical vocabulary
- Orally rehearse explanations
- Play word and language games to practise using 'explanation'-type words/phrases in context
- Begin to plan new text and use drama/role play to explore sections
- Make decisions about layout then complete plan

Phase 2 outcome

To have planned my own explanation text

PHASE 3

- Shared write introduction
- Children write own independently
- Shared write first paragraph
- Children write own independently
- Continue in this way until children complete the main body of their explanations
- Shared write conclusion
- Children write own independently
- Mark, feed back and edit
- Turn polished piece into a designed final explanation text
- Publish and share
- Evaluate

UNIT PLAN

Theme: *Pandora Discovered* – **Narrative**   Upper Key Stage 2

FINAL OUTCOME
To write a myth that is set on Pandora

PHASE 1

- Shared read a range of short myths, respond – likes, dislikes, puzzles, patterns
- Collect language and vocabulary that are effective
- Use a map or story mountain to outline the basic plot of a myth
- Immerse children in myths so that they internalise the language patterns and vocabulary
- Collect list of writer's hints
- Hook – watch *Pandora Discovered* and begin to consider myths that might have come from the planet

Phase 1 outcome
To know what a good myth looks and sounds like (plot and language)

PHASE 2

- Focus the children on an aspect of *Pandora Discovered* that is engaging them (e.g. the bioluminescence of some creatures/plants)
- Use drama to explore how this can have come about: What were the events that led to this? Who was responsible?
- Support children to use elements of the myths read in phase 1 to help them to create new stories
- Use the story map or mountain to begin to plan ideas
- Use oral rehearsal and further drama activities to check key events and mythical qualities of the evolving stories
- Support children to plan how they will incorporate elements on the writer's hints list
- Finalise plan

Phase 2 outcome
To have planned my myth

PHASE 3

- Shared write opening to get the writing process started
- Children independently write the opening and build-up paragraphs
- Mark and follow up on issues before they move onto the problem and resolution parts
- Shared write to support, where necessary
- Children independently write rest of story
- Support them to edit and refine story
- Share and evaluate

UNIT PLAN

Theme: *Pandora Discovered* – **Persuasive setting description**   Upper Key Stage 2

FINAL OUTCOME

To write setting descriptions of Pandora for a travel brochure

PHASE 1

- Shared read a range of setting descriptions (including travel brochure descriptions)
- Explore and respond: Which do you prefer and why? Identify audience and purpose for each
- Begin to collect writer's hints
- Identify features of persuasive descriptions
- Explore the use of expanded noun phrases; metaphors, onomatopoeia, alliteration to add detail and effect
- Collect and 'play with' effects found in travel brochures including persuasive voice
- Chunk a typical brochure description to get a feel for structure

Phase 1 outcome

To know what good setting descriptions/ travel brochure pieces sound like

PHASE 2

- Play barrier games to support with clarity of descriptions
- Hook – watch *Pandora Discovered* and use stills from the film to help children to choose stimulus for writing own description
- Play word and language games to support with finding appropriate noun phrases, metaphors, onomatopoeia and alliteration to describe settings
- Orally rehearse – support with adding persuasive voice
- Complete plan (bear in mind audience and purpose)

Phase 2 outcome

To have planned my own persuasive setting description

PHASE 3

- Model how to use plan to write opening of setting description
- Children write opening independently
- Mark and either model next part or children proceed with writing the rest of their descriptions independently
- Read descriptions aloud in order to support with editing
- Refine and publish
- Evaluate

Instructions
Spy themed: how to travel incognito, using a spy's toolkit, how to spy on a target; invent spy gadgets and write instructions for them; how to avoid pigeons

Description
Freeze-frame and describe the action at key moments; character descriptions

Pigeon: Impossible

available at: www.youtube.com/ watch?v=ZDtb LIzhS7A

Narrative
Write the story of the film; stop the action when the pigeon presses the button and write the ending; write a prequel (another mission foiled by the pigeon)

Recount
Newspaper report of the failed mission; eyewitness reports of the events; first person account of the events (pigeon and spy)

UNIT PLAN

Theme: *Pigeon: Impossible* – **Instructions**   Lower Key Stage 2

FINAL OUTCOME
To write a set of instructions for using a new spy gadget

PHASE 1

- Hook – watch *Pigeon: Impossible*
- Explain task – to make up, and then write a set of instructions for, a new spy gadget
- Shared read various sets of instructions
- Explore and respond – compare and contrast
- Identify the features and typical language of instructions (e.g. introduction, what you need, what you do, bossy verbs, ordered steps, concluding statement)
- Collect writer's hints for instructions
- Play language games to develop understanding of bossy verb meanings (e.g. mime the action)
- Chunk text into sections and discuss layout (purpose)

Phase 1 outcome
To know what a good set of instructions looks and sounds like

PHASE 2

- Watch or read *Wallace & Gromit Cracking Contraptions* (www.youtube.com/watch?v=d54yH2sNpw4)
- Children design new spy gadget
- Research James Bond's gadgets to feed the children's ideas
- Children sketch and label their new gadget, and explain it
- Begin to plan new set of instructions
- Talk games to generate ideas for the introduction, and the 'what you need' section
- Talk activities to support with ideas for adding detail into each step and support with ideas for a concluding statement
- Complete plan

Phase 2 outcome
To have planned my instructions

PHASE 3

- Shared write introduction
- Children write introduction and 'what you need' independently
- Shared write initial steps
- Children write steps independently
- Shared write concluding statement
- Children complete independently
- Mark, feed back and edit
- Publish and share
- Evaluate

UNIT PLAN

Theme: *Pigeon: Impossible* – Narrative   Lower Key Stage 2

FINAL OUTCOME

To write *Pigeon: Impossible 2* (a sequel)

PHASE 1

- Hook – watch *Pigeon: Impossible* and respond (likes, dislikes, puzzles, patterns)
- Explain task: to write a sequel (a new event that fails due to the pigeon)
- Use mapping to identify the key events in *Pigeon: Impossible*, check children's understanding of the plot
- Read a range of short stories with similar plot patterns (repeated problem/resolution)
- Collect language and vocabulary that are effective
- Collect list of writer's hints

Phase 1 outcome

To know and understand the *Pigeon: Impossible* story and what makes a good repeated problem/resolution story

PHASE 2

- Watch clips from the *Johnny English* films to help children think through the kinds of tasks that spies get asked to do
- Use drama and role play to guide thinking through main parts to new story: What is his mission? How does the pigeon get in the way? What three things happen (e.g. building being blown up, big car smash, etc.)? How is it resolved? How does it end?
- Create individual story maps and then turn into a plan
- Use oral rehearsal and further drama activities to check that the planned story is going to have the desired impact on the audience
- Support children to plan how they will incorporate language and vocabulary collected in phase 1

Phase 2 outcome

To have planned my sequel to *Pigeon: Impossible*

PHASE 3

- Shared write opening to get the writing process started
- Children independently write the opening and build-up paragraphs
- Mark and follow up on issues before they move onto the problem and resolution parts
- Shared write to support, where necessary
- Children independently write problems/resolutions
- Shared/independently write story ending
- Support them to edit and refine story
- Share and evaluate
- Publish

UNIT PLAN

<u>Theme</u>: ***Pigeon: Impossible*** **– Newspaper reports**

Lower Key Stage 2

FINAL OUTCOME

Newspaper report based on the events of *Pigeon: Impossible*

PHASE 1

- Hook – watch *Pigeon: Impossible* and respond (likes, dislikes, puzzles, patterns)
- Ask the children: If you were a TV news producer, what would you have put into an item about the *Pigeon: Impossible* events? Children role-play ideas
- General discussion re: news of this nature: Audience? Purpose? How it is handled; sensationalism
- Shared read age-appropriate newspaper reports and respond
- Immerse children in newspaper reports so that they internalise the language patterns
- Collect list of writer's hints, and appropriate vocabulary
- Chunk newspaper report into sections to check understanding of typical structure (headline, '5 W's intro para, story para, background/eyewitness para, concluding para)

Phase 1 outcome

To know what a good newspaper report looks and sounds like

PHASE 2

- Explain task and watch *Pigeon: Impossible*
- Explore key events through drama/freeze-framing
- Hot-seat characters and other parties (e.g. eyewitnesses, police) to collect and develop ideas
- Use chunks from phase 1 to plan own report
- Explore headline to use
- Play language games to practise the effective use of journalistic language
- Orally rehearse report section by section
- Finalise plan

Phase 2 outcome

To have planned my newspaper report

PHASE 3

- Shared write opening, including headline and use of language
- Independent and guided write openings
- Shared write next parts, picking up on issues as report progresses
- Support with concluding paragraph – check it has impact
- Peer evaluate success, then edit
- Publish

Information
Tribal rituals; people of the rainforests; rainforest environments; rainforest animals; endangered species

Description
Settings; animals; tribal characters; describe the action at key moments

Ride of Passage

available at:
www.youtube.com/
watch?v=29fl
Glr0cuQ

Narrative
Write the story of the film; stop the action as Toki is cutting the chameleon free and write the ending; write the dialogue for key moments; retell the story as if you were the chameleon

Recount
Newspaper report of the events; eyewitness reports (from the animals and humans involved); diary entries

Persuasion
Debate the use of animals for this ritual; leaflets about dying rainforests; letters to persuade

UNIT PLAN

Theme: *Ride of Passage* – Information   Lower Key Stage 2

PHASE 1

- Shared read a variety of information leaflets (persuasive)
- Compare and contrast; explore and respond – likes, dislikes, puzzles, patterns; and identify purpose and audience of each
- Begin to collect writer's hints (including persuasive techniques)
- Immerse the children in information leaflets so that they internalise the language patterns
- Collect effective language and vocabulary
- Chunk an information leaflet into sections to analyse structure, check understanding of purpose of each section

Phase 1 outcome

To know what a good information leaflet looks and sounds like

PHASE 2

- Hook – watch *Ride of Passage*
- Establish what children know about endangered animals
- Use a variety of information texts to develop content for information leaflets – keep information simple and focused (e.g. two endangered animals)
- Use word and language games to check understanding of technical vocabulary; and of persuasive devices appropriate to information leaflets
- Support children to create new plan: introduction; two key sections (e.g. one per animal); conclusion; discuss and orally rehearse ideas; add these to plan
- Consider layout – children to know what their leaflet will look like
- Finalise plan

Phase 2 outcome

To have planned my information leaflet

PHASE 3

- Shared write intro paragraph
- Children independently write introductory paragraph
- Edit and refine
- In turn, shared write, children independently write, edit and refine next two sections
- Shared/independently write conclusion
- Decide on layout of final text – add pictures etc.
- Refine to check for impact on reader
- Share with audience and evaluate

UNIT PLAN

Theme: *Ride of Passage* – Narrative (dialogue)   Lower Key Stage 2

FINAL OUTCOME

To write dialogue based on *Ride of Passage*

PHASE 1

- Look at stills or pictures from key moments in well-known stories or films and ask children to tell you (guess) what the people are saying
- Explain the term 'dialogue' and play talk games that involve the children inventing (or retelling) dialogue
- Using the original stills or pictures focus on what the dialogue tells us about the characters who are speaking; now do the same activity but without visual images – listening to dialogue – what do we learn about characters?
- Ensure that children know the conventions for writing dialogue; practise this if necessary
- Focus on vocabulary that tells us more about how the speech is said (e.g. whispered, shouted); play drama games to explore this and word games to embed new vocabulary
- Collect list of writer's hints for dialogue

Phase 1 outcome

To know how dialogue is used to tell us more about characters in stories

PHASE 2

- Hook – watch *Ride of Passage*
- Freeze-frame and use role play to imagine what the characters might be saying
- Develop this so that what they are saying is telling us something about how the characters are feeling
- Do this for several different scenes from *Ride of Passage*
- Choose a scene and plan your dialogue
- Act it out – check it works and orally rehearse it

Phase 2 outcome

To have planned my dialogue

PHASE 3

- Shared write opening to check understanding
- Children independently write their dialogue
- Polish
- Publish (could be recorded and played 'over' the film)

UNIT PLAN

Theme: *Ride of Passage* – **Persuasion**   Lower Key Stage 2

FINAL OUTCOME
Persuasive letter based on *Ride of Passage*.

PHASE 1

- Hook – watch *Ride of Passage* and read letter from Toki asking the children to help him to persuade his tribe to stop killing animals
- General discussion: What is persuasion? Talk activities to support children with understanding
- Shared read a variety of persuasive letters
- Discuss purpose and audience; compare and contrast – which work best and why?
- Identify use of language, collect and check understanding of what makes it effective
- Collect list of writer's hints for letters of persuasion
- Chunk a persuasive letter into sections
- Recap understanding of layout of letters

Phase 1 outcome

To know what a good persuasive letter looks and sounds like

PHASE 2

- Use drama/role play to explore the arguments against killing animals; collect ideas
- Group ideas into themes and generate persuasive sentences – orally rehearse to check that they sound right and have the right effect
- Check children are clear about purpose and audience for letter
- Use chunks from phase 1 to plan new letter
- Take elements from the list of writer's hints and practise using them as part of the arguments
- Orally rehearse each section of the letter
- Add effective vocabulary to plan

Phase 2 outcome

To have planned my persuasive letter

PHASE 3

- Shared write opening of letter – model how to use plan
- Children independently write the opening
- Mark and follow up on issues before they move onto the main body of the letter
- Shared write to support with main body and closing
- Children independently write rest of letter
- Support them to edit and refine whole text
- Publish, share and evaluate
- Send letters to Toki's elders!

Information
Great Train Robbery 1963:
Who was involved? What happened?
Where are they now? Write own
information text about Frank
and Jason's robbery

Description
Settings; rubies; train travel
(link to poetry); simile
and metaphor

Ruckus

available at:
https://vimeo.com/
68344409

Narrative
Write the story of the film;
stop the action as they fall from
the train and write the ending;
write a prequel (another
robbery)

Poetry
Possible themes: desert,
trains, transport, escape,
jewels, feelings

Recount
Newspaper report of
the robbery; eyewitness report
of the events; first-
person account of the
events

UNIT PLAN

Theme: *Ruckus* – **Information**

Lower Key Stage 2

FINAL OUTCOME

Non-chronological report about the Great Train Robbery of 1963

PHASE 1

- Hook – watch *Ruckus*, ask children if they have ever heard of anyone else stealing jewels (or similar) from a train
- Watch/look at Great Train Robbery news reports (film/paper) and collect and mind map children's questions about the robbery (e.g. Who did it? Why? Have they been caught? Are they still alive? What happened to the money that they stole?)
- Chunk a simple non-chronological report (e.g. from a double-page spread in a children's reference book on history) to establish the structure of a report
- Immerse children in the text type by reading and analysing other non-chronological reports
- Identify key features and collect effective language and vocabulary
- Collect writer's hints

Phase 1 outcome

I know what a good non-chronological report looks and sounds like

PHASE 2

- Using a model text as a frame, decide on the key paragraphs of the report (use areas that the children have identified)
- Children research the key areas – support them to generate their own plan, making sure that there is enough information for each paragraph
- Orally rehearse use of appropriate and effective language
- Use model text to support children to make design decisions: What will their report look like on the page? Are they going to add any pictures? Where will they go? Why?
- Finalise plan

Phase 2 outcome

To have planned my non-chronological report

PHASE 3

- Shared write opening paragraph – model how to use the plan as a guide
- Independent and guided write opening paragraphs
- Shared write next parts picking up on issues as report progresses
- Support with polishing final draft, including design decisions (add pictures if required)
- Edit and evaluate
- Publish

UNIT PLAN

Theme: *Ruckus* – **Narrative**   Lower Key Stage 2

FINAL OUTCOME
To write a prequel to *Ruckus*

PHASE 1

- Read a range of short stories with robbery as the key theme
- Explore purpose and audience for each
- Explore likes, dislikes, puzzles, patterns for each
- Collect language and vocabulary that are effective
- Use mapping to identify typical plot structure to these types of stories (i.e. opening, build-up, problem, resolution, ending)
- Check that children are clear about 'suspense', which is usually used in the build-up and problem parts – explore this if necessary – using language games
- Collect items for writer's hints list – tools that make a robbery story effective?

Phase 1 outcome

To know and understand what a good robbery story looks and sounds like (plot and language)

PHASE 2

- Hook – watch *Ruckus*
- Support children to think about a back story for Frank and Jason: Who are they? Have they always been robbers? Why? What else have they stolen? Have they got away with their crimes?
- Introduce second hook: fictional news article about a jewel thief – setting etc. to be clear so that children are only having to make up the plot to new story
- Use drama and role play to guide thinking through five main parts to new story
- Create individual story maps and then use to create a plan
- Use oral rehearsal and further drama activities to check that the planned story will have the desired impact on the audience
- Support children to plan how they will incorporate language and suspense devices from writer's hints

Phase 2 outcome

To have planned my robbery story

PHASE 3

- Shared write opening to get the writing process started
- Children independently write the opening and build up paragraphs
- Mark and follow up on issues before they move onto the problem and resolution parts
- Shared write to support, where necessary
- Children independently write rest of story
- Support them to edit and refine story
- Share and evaluate

UNIT PLAN

Theme: *Ruckus* – **Newspaper reports**   Lower Key Stage 1

FINAL OUTCOME
Newspaper report 'Jewel Thieves in Near Death Experience!'

PHASE 1

- Hook – Great Train Robbery news reports (film/paper)
- General discussion re: news of this nature: Audience? Purpose? How it is handled; sensationalism
- Shared read age-appropriate newspaper reports and respond
- Immerse children in newspaper reports so that they internalise the language patterns
- Collect list of writer's hints, and appropriate vocabulary
- Chunk newspaper report into sections to check understanding of typical structure (headline, '5 W's intro para, story para, background/eyewitness para, concluding para)

Phase 1 outcome
To know what a good newspaper report looks and sounds like

PHASE 2

- Introduce stimulus by watching *Ruckus*
- Explore key events through drama/freeze-framing
- Hot-seat characters and other parties (e.g. train driver, police, doctors, owner of the ruby) to collect and develop ideas
- Use chunks from phase 1 to plan own report
- Explore headline to use
- Orally rehearse use of journalistic language; record key ideas

Phase 2 outcome
To have planned my newspaper report

PHASE 3

- Shared write opening, including headline and use of language
- Independent and guided write openings
- Shared write next parts picking up on issues as report progresses
- Support with concluding paragraph – check it has impact
- Peer evaluate success, then edit
- Publish

Recount
Lighthouse keeper's diary;
newspaper reports of events;
eyewitness reports; biography of
the lighthouse keeper

Description
Settings: lighthouses, stormy seas,
stormy night, village scene

Lighthouse

available at:
www.youtube.com/
watch?v=6HfB
bSUORvo

Narrative
Write the story of the film;
write the opening (suspense);
stop the action when the light
breaks and write the ending;
write the story from the point
of view of a villager; change
the ending

Explanation
How lighthouses work; how
the lighthouse keeper stopped
the boat from hitting the rocks;
other people who help us
and how

UNIT PLAN

Theme: *Lighthouse* – Explanation   Lower Key Stage 2

FINAL OUTCOME

To write an explanation of how the lighthouse keeper stopped the boat from hitting the rocks

PHASE 1

- Shared read explanation texts
- Explore and respond, and discuss purpose and audience
- Begin to collect writer's hints
- Immerse children in explanation texts (e.g. 'How kites fly?') so that they internalise the language
- Unpick language features and understand why they are used/effective
- Build word bank of technical vocabulary (short write glossary) and other 'explanation'-type words/phrases
- Direct teach around the structure of the explanation text – heading, introduction, paragraph content, conclusion, diagrams/pictures
- Discuss layout (purpose)
- Finalise list of writer's hints

Phase 1 outcome

To know what a good explanation text looks and sounds like

PHASE 2

- Hook – watch *Lighthouse* and introduce explanation task
- Use hook and picture/video stimulus to discuss technical vocabulary needed for writing explanation
- Begin to build list of technical vocabulary
- Play word and language games to practise using 'explanation'-type words/phrases in context
- Use chunks from phase 1 to begin planning and use drama/role play to explore sections
- Develop plan, including technical vocabulary to be used
- Make decisions about layout – what goes where on the page and why?

Phase 2 outcome

To have planned my own explanation text

PHASE 3

- Model write introduction
- Children write own
- Shared write first paragraph
- Children write own
- Support with decisions about next paragraph, including layout
- Children complete the rest of their explanations
- Mark, feed back and edit
- Publish and share
- Evaluate

UNIT PLAN

Theme: *Lighthouse* – **Narrative**   Lower Key Stage 2

FINAL OUTCOME
To write the opening narrative for *Lighthouse*

PHASE 1

- Watch openings/build-ups of short spooky/suspense films, respond to and analyse (likes, dislikes, puzzles, patterns)
- Read a range of short spooky/suspense stories, respond to and analyse openings/build-up (likes, dislikes, puzzles, patterns)
- Collect language and vocabulary that are effective
- Collect list of writer's hints – tools/writerly tricks that make an opening really effective
- Use mapping to identify typical pattern of openings/build-up

Phase 1 outcome
To know what a good suspenseful opening sounds like

PHASE 2

- Hook – watch *Lighthouse* to the point where the light goes out
- Support children to think about what an author might have written to narrate the events of the opening
- Use drama and role play to guide thinking through the main events; collect vocabulary and language
- Use oral rehearsal and further drama activities to clarify thinking, weave ideas from writer's hints into events and to check that the opening is going to have the desired impact on the audience
- Create plan – support children to plan how they will incorporate vocabulary, language and suspense devices

Phase 2 outcome
To have planned my own suspenseful opening

PHASE 3

- Shared write the first part of the opening to get the writing process started
- Children independently write
- Mark and follow up on issues before they move onto completing their openings and build-up
- Shared write to support, where necessary
- Support them to edit and refine
- Share and evaluate
- Publish

UNIT PLAN

Theme: *Lighthouse* – Recount (diary)   Lower Key Stage 2

FINAL OUTCOME
To write a diary entry of the events in *Lighthouse*

PHASE 1

- Shared read diary entries/extracts (avoid ones that are too informal – remember that these are models for writing)
- Compare and contrast; explore and respond – likes, dislikes, puzzles, patterns; and identify purpose of each
- Immerse the children in short diary entries (need to be eventful like the lighthouse keeper's one is going to be!) so that they internalise the language structures
- Collect list of writer's hints for diaries (avoid an overemphasis on 'informal language')
- Chunk a diary entry into parts to support with structure
- Hook – watch *Lighthouse* and respond (likes, dislikes, puzzles, patterns)

Phase 1 outcome
To know what a good diary entry sounds like

PHASE 2

- Support the children to sequence and map the main events from the film
- Use freeze-framing to add detail to each event (e.g. the thunder crashed above, the waves smashed below)
- Collect vocabulary (including time words to structure the recount)
- Use the map to help plan their new diary entries
- Play word/language games to orally rehearse the use of time words and the use of vocabulary to add detail – children add these to their plan

Phase 2 outcome
To have planned my diary entry

PHASE 3

- Shared write opening of diary entry – model how to use plan
- Children independently write the opening
- Mark and follow up on issues before they move onto the main body of the diary entry
- Shared write to support with main body and closing
- Children independently write rest of diary entry
- Support them to edit and refine whole text
- Publish, share and evaluate

Recount
Diary entries about war, his wife;
letters to and from his wife, the child;
autobiography

Description
The piano; the trenches;
characters past and present; his
home past and present

The Piano

available at:
www.youtube.com/
watch?v=-ZJDN
Sp1QJA

Narrative
Write the story of the film;
write a prequel; freeze-frame and
write stories from key moments;
write a stream of consciousness;
write dialogue between
characters (play script)

Poetry
Possible themes: memories,
war, love, relationships,
growing old, music

UNIT PLAN

Theme: *The Piano* – Play script   Upper Key Stage 2

FINAL OUTCOME
To write a play script based on the war scene in *The Piano*

PHASE 1

- Hook – watch *The Piano* and respond (likes, dislikes, puzzles, patterns)
- Explain task
- Shared read a range of short scripts
- Respond (likes, dislikes, puzzles, patterns); compare and contrast
- Try reading/performing scripts with adverbs and stage directions removed – discuss effect; put in own; perform
- Use mapping to learn the key elements of a play script (e.g. narrator sets scene; character; colon – adverb/direction)
- Build writer's hints list for play scripts

Phase 1 outcome

To know what a good play script looks and sounds like

PHASE 2

- Watch clips from *The Piano* and use stills to generate ideas for the events that he is recalling
- Use drama and freeze-framing to support children to think through what happened, and what the two characters might be saying
- Storyboard the short scene and add speech bubbles (could use app such as Comic Life)
- Orally rehearse ideas to focus on adverbs for being precise – showing the reader *how* the words are to be read
- Develop narrator's introduction – draft, think, orally rehearse
- Finalise plan

Phase 2 outcome

To have planned my play script

PHASE 3

- Children draft narrator's introduction
- Mark and feed back; redraft if necessary
- Model write play script opening and recap expectations around use of precise language
- Children write own
- Perform and evaluate
- Edit
- Perform

UNIT PLAN

Theme: **The Piano – Poetry (free verse)**   Upper Key Stage 2

PHASE 1

- Read a range of war-themed poems, respond (likes, dislikes, puzzles, patterns) and compare and contrast – which do you prefer and why?
- Explore and collect devices that are effective – metaphor, personification; check children understand how they are used; play language games to consolidate understanding
- Learn a list poem by heart
- Collect writer's hints for an effective list poem
- Expand vocabulary by generating synonyms for feelings, colours and size (e.g. heartbroken instead of sad; 'emerald' instead of 'green')
- Collect effective vocabulary and language, including personification and metaphors

Phase 1 outcome

To know what a list poem is and how personification can be used for effect

PHASE 2

- Hook – watch *The Piano* and respond (likes, dislikes, puzzles, patterns)
- Explain task – to write a poem about what a soldier might have in his pocket
- Use artefacts to develop ideas (e.g. handkerchief, key, bar of chocolate)
- Use talk games to explore abstract ideas for what could be in a soldier's pocket (e.g. my memories, the image of my mother, etc.)
- Make sure that the writer's hints are explored and rehearsed
- Plan poem

Phase 2 outcome

To have planned my poem

PHASE 3

- Model how to use plan to write beginning of poem
- Children write their poems
- Edit
- Publish and perform poems
- Evaluate them

UNIT PLAN

Theme: *The Piano* – Recount (diary)   Upper Key Stage 2

FINAL OUTCOME

To write a diary entry inspired by *The Piano*

PHASE 1

- Hook – watch *The Piano* and respond (likes, dislikes, puzzles, patterns)
- Explain task – to write his wife's diary entry from wartime
- Shared read diary entries/extracts (avoid ones that are too informal – remember that these are models for writing)
- Compare and contrast; explore and respond – likes, dislikes, puzzles, patterns; and identify purpose of each
- Build a list of writer's hints for diaries (avoid an overemphasis on 'informal language')
- Chunk a diary entry into parts to support with structure

Phase 1 outcome

To know what a good diary entry sounds like

PHASE 2

- Watch clips from *The Piano* and use stills to generate ideas for the events that she is recalling
- Use drama and freeze-framing to support children to think through what might have happened to her while he was at war, and how she might have been feeling
- Start to plan
- Play word/language games to orally rehearse the effective use of vocabulary to add detail (her personal feelings and recollections) – children add new ideas to their plan
- Orally rehearse ideas, being careful to weave in writer's hints
- Finalise plan

Phase 2 outcome

To have planned my diary entry

PHASE 3

- Shared write opening of diary entry – model how to use plan
- Children independently write the opening
- Mark and follow up on issues before they move onto the main body of the diary entry
- Shared write to support with main body and closing
- Children independently write rest of diary entry
- Support them to edit and refine whole text
- Publish, share and evaluate

Information
Recycling; upcycling; poverty; homelessness; children from around the world who work on trash heaps

Description
Settings: the junkyard, her house, specific objects; main character

Treasure

available at:
www.youtube.
com/watch?
v=PjgxCZnzGLQ

Narrative
Write the story of the film; stop the action when she finds the ring and write the ending; write a prequel (why is she there?); write a sequel

Explanation
How she came to live in a junkyard; recycling; upcycling; one person's junk is another person's treasure; what is a home?

Discussion
Is she happy? Should she return the ring to its owner? Are junkyards necessary?

UNIT PLAN

Theme: *Treasure* – Setting description   Key Stage 2

FINAL OUTCOME

To write a setting description of Esther's home

PHASE 1

- Hook – watch *Treasure*
- Explain task
- Establish what children know about 'settings' and how to describe them
- Shared read setting descriptions
- Compare and contrast; explore and respond – likes, dislikes, puzzles, patterns; and identify purpose and audience of each
- Immerse children in setting descriptions so that they internalise the language structures
- Collect writer's hints and effective vocabulary
- Play word/language games to develop the language of description
- Chunk a setting description into parts so that children understand structure
- Play word/language games to develop the language of description (use short film clips as stimulus)

Phase 1 outcome

To know what a good setting description sounds like

PHASE 2

- Watch *Treasure* again
- Use stills from this, and other similar picture stimulus, to generate ideas and vocabulary for the setting – remember to make it multisensory
- Support the children to create a new plan for the setting description (e.g. journey from one side to the other or from bottom to top)
- Pair work – children 'talk' their descriptions
- Play word/language games to continue to develop and rehearse the language of description (must be precise and appropriate for Esther's home)

Phase 2 outcome

To have planned my setting description

PHASE 3

- Model write first couple of lines
- Children independently write their descriptions
- Share and refine
- Publish by performing them with film stills/pictures as a backdrop
- Evaluate

UNIT PLAN

Theme: *Treasure* – Discussion   Key Stage 2

FINAL OUTCOME
To write a discussion about whether Esther should return the ring

PHASE 1

- Read a range of discussion texts
- Explore purpose and audience for each
- Use talk activities to further explore the concept of 'discussion'
- Collect list of writer's hints
- Play language games to practise using discursive language
- Chunk a discursive text into sections to clarify structure of discussion texts (paragraphs: intro, points for, points against, conclusion)

Phase 1 outcome
To know what a good discussion text looks and sounds like

PHASE 2

- Hook – watch *Treasure*
- Introduce task: discussion 'Should Esther return the ring?' Hold an initial class discussion on this
- Use discussion-based role-play and drama games (e.g. conscience alley) to explore reasons for and against returning the ring
- Use chunks from phase 1 to help to plan new discussion
- Use language games to further explore the effective use of discursive language, and other aspects on the writer's hints list
- Orally rehearse possible introductions/conclusions to this discussion
- Complete plan

Phase 2 outcome
To have planned my own discussion text

PHASE 3

- Shared write introduction and points for paragraph
- Children independently write introduction and points for paragraph
- Shared write points against and concluding paragraphs
- Children independently write points against and concluding paragraphs
- Support with editing and refining discussions
- Share and evaluate
- Publish

UNIT PLAN

Theme: *Treasure* – Narrative   Key Stage 2

PHASE 1

- Watch *Treasure* and respond (likes, dislikes, puzzles, patterns)
- Use freeze-framing to map the key events of the story: opening; collects items: car; tree, jewellery box, ring; home: sets up new items; ending
- Use storyboard, mountain or map as a visual prompt to the key events
- Shared read stories with similar plot patterns
- Explore and respond – likes, dislikes, puzzles, patterns
- Collect effective language and vocabulary
- Collect list of writer's hints

Phase 1 outcome

To know the plot of *Treasure* and be familiar with the language used in other similar stories

PHASE 2

- Use storyboard created in phase 1 to guide children to plan their stories of the film
- Role-play the opening; orally rehearse sentences
- Then take each section and role-play; collect vocabulary around: setting, objects she finds and Esther's thoughts/feelings
- Use word/language games to explore and develop precise and effective vocabulary
- Orally rehearse new ideas and practise using elements from the writer's hints
- Finalise plan

Phase 2 outcome

To have planned my *Treasure* story

PHASE 3

- Show children what their final published story will look like (e.g. typed, class storybook, etc.)
- Model write opening – using plan
- Children write opening independently
- Model write main events – using plan
- Children write main events independently
- Model write ending – using plan
- Children write ending independently
- Mark, feed back and edit
- Publish and share

References

Barrs, M. and Cork, V. (2001) *The Reader in the Writer*, London: Centre for Language in Primary Education.

Chambers, A. (1993) *Tell Me: Children Reading and Talk*, Gloucester: Thimble Press.

Corbett, P. (2008) *Talk for Writing in Practice: The Teaching Sequence for Writing*, 00467–2008PDF-EN-21, London: HMSO.

Corbett (2012) 'Teaching literacy across the curriculum with a focus on non-fiction', National Literacy Trust conference proceedings, Manchester.

Department for Education (2013) *The National Curriculum in England Key Stages 1 and 2 framework*. London: DfE.

Dudley, P. (2011) 'Lessons for learning: how teachers learn in contexts of lesson study', unpublished doctoral thesis, University of Cambridge.

Fisher, R., Myhill, D., Jones, S. and Larkin, S. (2010) *Using Talk to Support Writing*, London: Sage.

Martin, A., Lovat, C. and Purnell, G. (2004) *The Really Useful Literacy Book: Being Creative with Literacy in the Primary Classroom*, 2nd edn, London: Routledge.

Ofsted (2011) *Excellence in English: What We Can Learn from 12 Outstanding Schools (100229)*, London: DfE.

The report of a joint research project carried out by UKLA/PNS (2004) *Raising Boys' Achievements in Writing*.

Internet

Assessment Reform Group (2002) www.aaia.org.uk/category/afl/

Parietti, K. (2013) www.theguardian.com/teacher-network/teacher-blog/2013/feb/01/teaching-creative-writing-ideas-activities-primary-literacy

Children's books

The Arrival by Shaun Tan (2006) Hodder Children's Books

Beegu by Alexis Deacon (2003) Red Fox

Bill's New Frock by Anne Fine (1989) Methuen

Charlie and the Chocolate Factory by Roald Dahl (1967) Puffin Books

Danny, the Champion of the World by Roald Dahl (1975) Puffin Books

A Dark, Dark Tale by Ruth Brown (1981) Andersen Press

The Fib and Other Stories by George Layton (2001) Pan Macmillan

The Firework Maker's Daughter by Philip Pullman (1995) Corgi Yearling Books

Grandpa Chatterji by Jamila Gavin (1993) Mammoth

The Hobbit by J.R.R. Tolkien (1937) Unwin Paperbacks

The Iron Man by Ted Hughes (1968) Faber & Faber

Kensuke's Kingdom by Michael Morpurgo (1999) Egmont

Lost and Found by Oliver Jeffers (2005) HarperCollins Children's Books

The Lost Happy Endings by Carol Ann Duffy and Jane Ray (2006) Bloomsbury

Meerkat Mail by Emily Gravett (2006) Macmillan Children's Books

Mirror by Jeannie Baker (2010) Walker Books

The Owl Who Was Afraid of the Dark by Jill Tomlinson (2000) Egmont Books

Tell Me a Dragon by Jackie Morris (2009) Frances Lincoln Children's Books

There's a Boy in the Girls' Bathroom by Louis Sachar (1987) Bloomsbury

Three Cheers for Inventors! by Marcia Williams (2005) Walker Books

Trash by Andy Mulligan (2010) David Fickling Books

Tuesday by David Wiesner (1999) Clarion Books

Voices in the Park by Anthony Browne (1998) Picture Corgi Books

Way Home by Libby Hathorn and Gregory Rogers (1994) Andersen Press

Weslandia by Paul Fleischman (2009) Candlewick Press

Who's Afraid? and Other Strange Stories by Philippa Pearce (1988) Penguin Group

The Worst Witch by Jill Murphy (1974) Penguin Books

Zoo by Anthony Browne (1994) Random House

Films

Alma: www.youtube.com/watch?v=tECaYQ1AzkM

Bubbles: https://vimeo.com/21510156

The Clocktower: www.youtube.com/watch?v=nMIOuPxhCVI

El Caminante: from the *British Film Institute: Story Shorts* DVD

The Girl with the Yellow Bag: https://vimeo.com/26261136

Lighthouse: www.youtube.com/watch?v=6HfBbSUORvo

Once in a Lifetime: https://vimeo.com/23805703

Pandora Discovered: www.youtube.com/watch?v=GBGDmin_38E

The Piano: www.youtube.com/watch?v=-ZJDNSp1QJA

Pigeon: Impossible: www.youtube.com/watch?v=ZDtbLIzhS7A

Ride of Passage: www.youtube.com/watch?v=29flGlr0cuQ

Ruckus: https://vimeo.com/68344409

Something Fishy: https://vimeo.com/24962214

Stray: www.youtube.com/watch?v=_l0lirEuP_8

Treasure: www.youtube.com/watch?v=PjgxCZnzGLQ

Wallace & Gromit Cracking Contraptions – The Snoozatron: www.youtube.com/watch?v=d54yH2sNpw4

Zahra: https://vimeo.com/23455377

A Quick guide to completing a gaps sheet

1   Identify the pupil who best represents the attainment group's strengths and weaknesses in writing.

2   Collect his or her assessment information (e.g. progress towards performance descriptors, or school's own system, or criterion scale) and approximately five pieces of recent, independent writing from a range of different text types.

3   Using your assessment grid, identify the broad areas of concern (i.e. which areas are not ticked/completed?).

4   For each concern, look over the writing samples to identify the key issue – remember that the more specific you are here, the more impact you are likely have on writing improvement.

5   Once you have recorded five or six key issues, decide on what you are going to teach to help develop these areas of learning (teaching objectives).

6   For each issue, decide on a child-friendly target (learning outcomes).

Blank gaps grid

B

Writing Gaps Grid

Class: _____   Date: _____

Group	Assessment	Next stage of learning	
	Issues	**Objectives**	**Key learning outcomes** (I can . . . , I know . . . , I understand . . .)
	Word structure/language	Word structure/language	
	Text structure	Text structure	
	Sentence construction and punctuation	Sentence construction and punctuation	

Gaps grids

C

Writing Gaps Grid

Class: Reception   Date: End of Summer Term

Group & level	Assessment	Next stage of learning	
	Issues	**Objectives**	**Key learning outcomes** (I can . . . , I know . . . , I understand . . .)
Expected	**Application of phonics/confidence in writing** • Sometimes reverse letters within phonemes (e.g. 'wo' instead of 'ow') • Develop quantity of writing (expectations)	**Application of phonics/confidence in writing** • Read back to check phonics applied correctly – visual representations • Develop quantity of writing produced	• I can read my writing to check my spelling
	Handwriting • Develop letter formation (e.g. reversal of bs and ds) • Use lines – write in a straight line • Remember to write left to right	**Handwriting** • Practise handwriting such that letters are correctly orientated; size is consistent and words are straight • Develop understanding of 'left to right'	• My handwriting is neat and careful
	Sentence/punctuation • Aware of caps and full stops but need to develop consistency of use • Need to use finger spaces to aid understanding of writing	**Sentence/punctuation** • Develop consistency of use of capital letters and full stop • Develop use of finger spaces	• I can use full stops and capital letters every time I write • I use finger spaces so that people can read my words

Writing Gaps Grid

Class: Reception
Date: End of Summer Term

Group & level	Assessment	Next stage of learning	
	Issues	**Objectives**	**Key learning outcomes** (I can . . . , I know . . . , I understand . . .)
Exceeding	**Application of phonics/vocabulary** • Application of Phase 5 phonics in writing • Check knowledge of second 200 *tricky* HFW • Use colour and size words (adjectives) to add information	**Application of phonics/vocabulary** • Teach visual representations of phonemes and apply in writing • Teach gaps from second 200 *tricky* HFW • Know and use adjectives to add detail	• I use my phonics to help me to spell correctly • I know all 30 tricky HFW • I can use adjectives in my sentences
	Text structure • Sequencing events • Use time words and numbers to organise	**Text structure** • Sequence real and imagined events • Know and use time words to organise events • Use numbers to organise non-fiction writing	• I can put events into the right order • I can use time words to organise events in my writing • I can use numbers to organise my writing
	Sentence/punctuation • Beginning to use exclamation and question marks • Beginning to use simple conjunctions to join ideas	**Sentence/punctuation** • Use of exclamation and question marks • Use of because, but, so to join ideas	• I can use exclamation and question mark • I can use because, but and so to join my ideas

Writing Gaps Grid

Class: Year 1   Date: End of Summer Term

Group & level	Assessment Issues	Next stage of learning Objectives	Key learning outcomes (I can . . . , I know . . . , I understand . . .)
Expected	**Word structure/language/text structure** • Words for effect/adventurous vocabulary is not developed • Not using devices to organise ideas in non-fiction writing (e.g. numbers, headings, bullet points) **Handwriting/spelling** • Develop letter formation and knowledge (e.g. reversal of bs and ds) • Knowledge of tricky HFW **Sentence construction and punctuation** • Sentences not always grammatically accurate (subject/verb agreement and irregular past tense verbs) • Capital letters and full stops not always accurate	**Word structure/language/text structure** • Know and use a range of adjectives to add detail • Use numbers, headings and bullet points to organise non-fiction writing **Handwriting/spelling** • Practise handwriting such that letters are correctly orientated and formed; know the difference between bs and ds and others • Build on existing knowledge of tricky HFW – know tricky words from all 300 **Sentence construction and punctuation** • Know subject/verb agreement • Know irregular past tense verb forms (e.g. catch → caught) • I know irregular past tense verb forms	• I can use adjectives to make my writing more interesting • I can use numbers, headings and bullet points to organise my non-fiction writing • I can form and orientate all of my letters correctly • I spell all of my tricky words correctly when I write • I can check that that the subject and verb in my sentences agree • Know how to check for accuracy of punctuation • Every time I write, I check that my punctuation is accurate

Writing Gaps Grid

Class: Year 2 Date: End of Summer Term

Group & level	Assessment — Issues	Next stage of learning — Objectives	Next stage of learning — Key learning outcomes (I can . . . , I know . . . , I understand . . .)
Expected	**Word structure/language** • Not enough detail in writing • Need to select words for effect **Text structure** • Openings and closings of whole text • Group ideas into sections **Sentence construction and punctuation** • Need to use exclamation marks, commas in lists and inverted commas • Need to extend sentences, use subordination	**Word structure/language** • Know and be able to use technical vocabulary • Know and be able to use a range of adjectives to add detail and for effect **Text structure** • Know how to start and end different types of writing • Group related material into paragraphs **Sentence construction and punctuation** • Use exclamation marks, question marks and commas in lists accurately • Use inverted commas • Write longer sentences; use subordination in relation to time and reason	**Word structure/language** • I can use topic words in my non-fiction writing • I use adjectives to make my writing more interesting to read **Text structure** • I can show the reader that my writing starts, and end it well • I can group my ideas into paragraphs **Sentence construction and punctuation** • I can use exclamation marks, question marks and commas in lists • I can use inverted commas to punctuate speech • I can write longer sentences, using time conjunctions and 'because' to join ideas

Writing Gaps Grid

Class: Year 3   Date: End of Summer Term

Group & level	Assessment		Next stage of learning	
	Issues		Objectives	Key learning outcomes (I can . . . , I know . . . , I understand . . .)
Expected	**Word structure/language/text structure** • Not using adjectives to elaborate on basic information • Attention to reader is not always clear		**Word structure/language/text structure** • Use of adjectives to expand sentences and add extra detail to nouns and descriptions • Use of rhetorical questions or use of humour to engage reader	• I can use adjectives in my sentences to add extra detail or information • I can use humour and questions to involve the reader in my writing
	Text structure • No links between sentences • Paragraphs often end abruptly		**Text structure** • Use adverbs and adverbial phrases or pronouns to refer back to something previously mentioned • Write closings to paragraphs, ensuring that a conclusion is drawn or a link is made	• I can use adverbs and adverbial phrases, as well as pronouns such as he/she/they/I/them, to make links between my sentences and refer back to something already mentioned • I can come to a conclusion of my main point at the end of a paragraph
	Sentence construction and punctuation • No variation in tense • Comma splicing		**Sentence construction and punctuation** • Vary tense by making comparisons such as 'Yesterday was sunny but today it is raining' • Know how to use commas to mark clauses	• I can compare the past to the present so that I have a variety of tenses in my writing • I can use commas correctly when linking clauses

Writing Gaps Grid

Class: Year 4   **Date:** End of Summer Term

Group & level	Assessment	Next stage of learning	
	Issues	**Objectives**	**Key learning outcomes** (I can . . ., I know . . ., I understand . . .)
Expected	**Word structure/language** • Adventurous vocabulary not used effectively – need to be selecting words for effect and using them accurately • Need to elaborate on basic information or events	**Word structure/language** • Know and use technical vocabulary in non-fiction and a range of effective adjectives and adverbs in all writing • Use planning to develop ideas about information or events	• I can use adventurous vocabulary accurately and to have a particular effect on the reader • I can use planning to help me to explain my ideas fully to the reader
	Text structure • Develop paragraphing – check content all related and clarity of links between sentences within paragraphs	**Text structure** • Organise text into paragraphs to distinguish between different information, events or processes • Use adverbs and conjunctions to establish cohesion within paragraphs	• I can use planning to make sure that the content of each paragraph is related • I can use adverbs and conjunctions to accurately join ideas within paragraphs
	Sentence construction and punctuation • Grammatical accuracy of sentences – consistency of tenses, forms of the verb, checking • Accuracy of punctuation and use of exclamation marks, question marks and speech marks	**Sentence construction and punctuation** • Compose grammatically accurate sentences paying particular attention to tenses and verb forms • Clarify meaning through the use of question marks and exclamation marks • Use of inverted commas • Use checking strategies for accuracy of punctuation	• I always 'write a bit, read a bit' to check that my sentences are accurate • I can use question marks, exclamation marks and inverted commas effectively • Every time I write, I check that my punctuation is correct

Writing Gaps Grid

Class: Year 5   **Date:** End of Summer Term

Group & level	Assessment	Next stage of learning	
	Issues	**Objectives**	**Key learning outcomes** (I can . . . , I know . . . , I understand . . .)
Expected	**Word structure/language** • Make deliberate vocabulary choices and use wider vocabulary to match topic • Need to use devices to address the reader	**Word structure/language** • Select words and language drawn from their knowledge of different texts (fiction and non-fiction) • Use questions/comments about events or characters to establish viewpoint	**Word structure/language** • I can use adventurous vocabulary accurately and appropriately • I can use questions/comments to show the reader how I feel about events or characters
	Text structure • Need to use paragraphs every time they write • Develop links within paragraphs and links between	**Text structure** • Use paragraphs to achieve pace and emphasis in narrative writing • Use planning to ensure that text is organised coherently	**Text structure** • In narrative writing, I can use paragraphs to emphasise important moments and move the action on • I can use planning to make sure that my paragraphs are organised to best effect
	Sentence construction and punctuation • Handle longer sentences more effectively • Improve accuracy of full range of punctuation • Develop speech punctuation	**Sentence construction and punctuation** • Know and use subordinate and relative clauses • Use punctuation to clarify meaning • Use speech punctuation accurately • Use checking strategies for accuracy of punctuation	**Sentence construction and punctuation** • I can use subordinate and relative clauses effectively • I can use the range of punctuation effectively, including speech punctuation • Every time I write, I check that my punctuation is correct and that it has the right effect on the reader

Writing Gaps Grid

Class: Year 6   Date: End of Summer Term

Group & level	Assessment		Next stage of learning
	Issues	Objectives	Key learning outcomes (I can . . . , I know . . . , I understand . . .)
Exceeding	**Word structure/language** • Appropriate style not always clearly established to maintain reader's interest • Use an increasingly wide vocabulary – make adventurous word choices though not always appropriate	**Word structure/language** • Use a range of devices to involve the reader • Know and be able to use words and language drawn from knowledge of text types	• I can adopt and maintain the appropriate style and use devices to involve the reader • I can use adventurous vocabulary effectively and accurately
	Text structure • Manage material across the whole text more effectively	**Text structure** • Organise ideas into a coherent set of paragraphs • In non-fiction writing, introduce, develop and conclude paragraphs appropriately	• I can use planning to make sure that my paragraphs are organised to best effect • Whenever I write, I introduce, develop and conclude paragraphs appropriately
	Sentence construction and punctuation • Use a wider range of conjunctions to clarify relationships between ideas • Use full range of punctuation for effect • Use colons, semicolons, brackets and dashes	**Sentence construction and punctuation** • Extend use and control of longer sentences by deploying a range of conjunctions effectively • Use punctuation to convey and clarify meaning • Use colons, semicolons, brackets and dashes	• I can use a wide range of effective and precise conjunctions to join my ideas • I can use the range of punctuation to create an effect and help the reader to understand my writing

D

Mind map
blank template

E Blank circles plan

UNIT PLAN	
Theme:	Key Stage

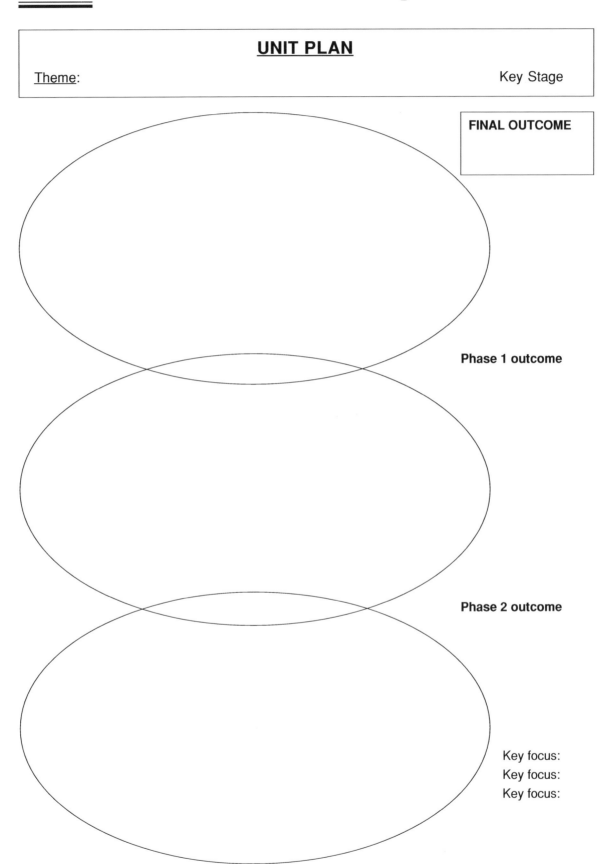

FINAL OUTCOME

Phase 1 outcome

Phase 2 outcome

Key focus:
Key focus:
Key focus:

F   Circles planning: quick guide

Step 1:	Decide on the text type that you want the children to produce. Complete the final outcome box (e.g. *Write an information leaflet*).
Step 2:	Choose the key focuses for this unit (from 'gaps' sheets; maximum of three) (e.g. *structure of text (paragraphing) and use of technical vocabulary*). Complete the 'key focus' boxes on right – each should say the same thing so that these are repeated three times.
Step 3:	Use the key focuses to add to the final outcome (e.g. Write an information leaflet *with a clear structure and technical vocabulary*).
Step 4:	Complete the outcome for Phase 1 (e.g. *I know what a good information leaflet looks and sounds like*).
Step 5:	Complete the outcome for Phase 2 (e.g. *I know what information will go into my leaflet and I have planned it out*).
Step 6:	List the activities that will be carried out during the three phases.
Step 7:	Go through and slot in 'key focus' teaching.
Step 8:	Go through and slot in short writing opportunities if necessary.
Step 9:	Plan the hook.
Consider: Audience and purpose for writing? Where will it be published?	
Long writes – opportunities to orchestrate all of the skills learnt and practise and consolidate across the curriculum.	

G   Synopsis of films

Film title	Suggested year groups	Summary of content
Bubbles	Key Stage 1	Fantasy setting – girl blows bubbles and goes for a ride in a bubbly world
The Clocktower	Key Stage 1	Fairy tale – a dancer turns the clockwork to make the clock tower work; when she stops, the world stops
The Girl with the Yellow Bag	Key Stage 1	Fantasy – girl picks up items and puts them into her yellow bag, the items fly out transformed
Once in a Lifetime	Key Stage 1/ Year 3	Fantasy – a man flies through the skies in his boat and he is joined by flying sea turtles
Something Fishy	Key Stage 1/ Year 3	Fantasy – girl in laundrette swims into the washing machine and has a fishy adventure
Stray	Key Stage 1	Line-drawn narrative about a dog who is injured and rescued by another dog
Zahra	Key Stage 1	Other cultures – set in a hot country, tells the story of a girl's attempts to water a dying plant
Lighthouse	Lower Key Stage 2	Suspense – the lighthouse has gone out, will the lighthouse keeper save the ship from crashing into the rocks?
Pigeon: Impossible	Lower Key Stage 2	Comedy/suspense – the story of what happens when a pigeon gets trapped in a secret agent's spy briefcase
Ride of Passage	Lower Key Stage 2	Other cultures – the story of Toki's quest to bring home the head of the biggest animal possible

Film title	Suggested year groups	Summary of content
Wallace & Gromit Cracking Contraptions – The Snoozatron	Lower Key Stage 2	Explanation/comedy – animated explanation of a machine that helps Wallace to sleep: the Snoozatron
El Caminante	Key Stage 2	Suspense – El Caminante is a tightrope walker, this is the story of his biggest challenge yet
Ruckus	Lower Key Stage 2	Adventure – the story of a great train robbery of epic proportions
Treasure	Key Stage 2	The story of a homeless woman searching through a junkyard, and what she finds
Alma	Upper Key Stage 2	Spooky – a little girl sees a familiar doll in a shop window; this is the story of what happens when she goes inside
Pandora Discovered	Upper Key Stage 2	Science fiction – spin-off from *Avatar*, a 'faction' film about the planet Pandora
The Piano	Upper Key Stage 2	Beautiful, multilayered narrative featuring an elderly man's recollections of the life that he has had

Index

Printed in Great Britain
by Amazon

84308849R00149